THEN GOD STEPPED IN

STORIES OF TRUE-LIFE MIRACLES

Dan and Susan Huntington

Soul Attitude Press

Cover photo by Andrew Small:
https://unsplash.com/photos/Lm6mqM_KqQY

Published by Soul Attitude Press
Pinellas Park, FL
www.soulattitudepress.com

ISBN 978-1-946338-63-1 (print without images)

ISBN 978-1-946338-62-4 (Kindle ebook)

ISBN 978-1-946338-61-7 (print with color images)

Printed in the United States of America
FIRST PRINTING

Contents

Introduction

Anybody who has ever opened the Bible, even the most casual reader or skeptic, has read of amazing miracles. We see in First Kings 17 how the ravens supplied food to Elijah, how the widow of Zarephath received an unending supply of meal and oil, and how Elijah raised her son from the dead. Or, in Exodus 17:7 how God supplied water to the children of Israel simply by commanding Moses to touch the rock with his staff, as well as receiving manna from heaven to feed the hungry Israelites as written in Exodus 16:15. The list goes on and on. In the New Testament we read stories of the lame walking, the blind seeing, lepers cleansed and people raised from the dead. These are all amazing miracles.

Today, I often hear the skeptics saying, "Those are some incredible miracles in that Bible of yours, but why don't we see them today? Is your God too busy to deal with today's traumatic issues?"

My answer is, I firmly believe that God performs miracles every day. The problem is, we don't look for miracles, nor do we ask for miracles. In today's culture we seem to depend on science or our own devices. God has not changed; but we have. We've become so self-centered, that we don't need help from anybody; we've got it all under control. However, if we open the eyes of our heart, we'll see miracles every day. Thus, the reason for writing this book.

The intent of this collection of true experiences is to offer hope and encouragement to those seeking spiritual answers. Like many Christians, you may be struggling with your faith. Doubts often creep into your mind. You may at times see yourself as an agnostic or maybe even call yourself an atheist. That is the evil one at work. This compilation of true stories, which are actually nothing short of amazing miracles, will hopefully get you thinking. However, if you are a born-again believer, this is an arsenal of information to use while sharing your faith. There is something here for everybody.

The Bible tells us that God is omnipresent.

Proverbs 15:3 says, *"the eyes of the Lord are in every place keeping watch on the evil and the good."* The Bible also tells us that God's timing is perfect. When Jesus' disciples were in a panic on a stormy sea, God did not immediately intervene. To test our faith, the Lord will often wait until a lesson is learned before he acts, like any good father would do. Proverbs 16:9 says, *"The heart of man plans his way, but the Lord establishes his steps."*

Has there ever been an event in your life where you can honestly say, "why am I still alive?" But for the grace of God, I, personally, should be in my grave. Not once, but three times in my seventy-nine years I have had such an experience. My stories, however, are only a small part of this book. This collection of events from these people's lives are real so I claim no literary ownership. The people sharing their miracles in this book see it as scattering seeds. The Bible says we are to go into all the world and proclaim the good news to all of creation. Matthew 13 speaks of a farmer who went out to sow and as he sowed, some seeds fell on the path and the birds came and ate them up. Other seeds fell on rocky ground where they did not have much soil, and they sprang up quickly, since they had no depth of soil. But when the sun rose, they were scorched and since they had no root they withered away. Other seeds fell among the thorns; the thorns grew up and choked them. Others fell on good soil and brought forth grain some hundred folds, some sixty, some thirty. Our fervent prayer is that our seeds fall on fertile soil. The beautiful photography has been included to depict God's miraculous handiwork.

1 Peter 3:15 says, *"But in your hearts honor Christ the Lord as holy, always being prepared to make a defense to anyone who asks you for a reason for the hope that is in you; yet do it with gentleness and respect."*

Acts 1:8 *"But you will receive power when the Holy Spirit has come upon you, and you will be my witnesses in Jerusalem and in all Judea and Samaria, and to the end of the earth."*

One hundred percent of the sale proceeds of this book will be donated to charity. Enjoy the testimonies and may God Bless you.

Dan H

Isaiah 55:8 "For my thoughts are not your thoughts, neither are your ways my ways declare the Lord."

December 23rd, 1941 at 3 AM, I was sleeping like a baby. As a matter-of-fact, I was a baby ten months old. For some unexplained reason my three-year-old brother Jimmy woke up and decided to get dressed; something he had never done before. Our cousin was on leave from the military and sleeping on the couch. Little Jimmy woke him saying, "Cuz, I can't get my shoes there's a big fire in the way." My cousin realized the house was engulfed in flames and yelled to my parents upstairs, "the house is on fire." This wood frame cottage was going up in flames like a tinderbox. The stairway collapsed in flames trapping the entire family upstairs. My father dropped my mother from the second story window into the arms of my cousin. He then ran to my sister's room only to see her bed fall through the floor. The same fate met my brothers Jack and Eddie. Their entire room was in flames when my dad finally pulled me from my crib and dropped me into my cousin's arms below. At that point my father passed out, falling out the window. He was hospitalized with third degree burns over eighty percent of his body, as well as a broken back. It's now Christmas eve and a family of seven was now a family of four. Seventy-nine years later, I'm the only survivor, and often wonder why God showed up for me, while my siblings perished. I believe they were the winners that day. For the last seventy-nine years Janet, Jack and Eddie have been resting in the arms of Jesus, while I still have work to do.

****

Fast forward to January 25th 1962 I'm a young married man with no kids. At approximately six o'clock in the afternoon, I had just arrived home, totally exhausted and looking forward to a much-needed nap. My wife was working at a local drugstore, so it was just me and Chico, our little Chihuahua. Although I'm a dog lover, I must admit I was not real fond of Chico. He was excitable, never stopped running and squeezing that little blue ball which drove me crazy. So that I could get some sleep, I considered putting Chico out on the screen porch but it was extremely cold that afternoon and I decided to keep him in the house. However, I did throw that squeaky blue ball outside. That little house was heated by a wood burning stove. I put a large log in the fire before retiring for my much-anticipated nap.

I was enjoying a deep dreamless sleep when suddenly I felt something scratching my face. I woke up immediately to come face-to-face with my little nemesis Chico. I could barely see his face, because the entire house was filled with smoke. Fortunately, I was still dressed. Picking up the Chihuahua, I ran out the door. I wasn't twenty yards away when I looked back and saw the entire house in flames. The firemen told me that opening the door gave oxygen to the fire which caused it to flame up. By the time the fire department arrived, the house had burned to the ground, and for the second time in my life, I escaped an inferno. Again, God showed up with perfect timing. A very interesting fact was, how did that little dog get up on the bed? It was something he had tried many times, but was never able to make it. Needless to say, that little rascal that used to irritate me to no end, became my best friend.

****

In 1999, my wife and I were enjoying the good life. We founded a food brokerage firm, and represented major food processors from around the country. We had a total of six salespeople working throughout the State of Florida. I was becoming a bit prideful and self-serving, thinking I had everything under control. The Bible says in Philippians 2:3 , "do nothing from selfish ambition or conceit, but in humility count others more significant than yourselves."

We had just been appointed to represent a large West Coast seafood processor. It was an excellent line and paid roughly $42,000 per year in commissions. With that additional income, I was able to hire another salesman for $40,000 per year salary. Shortly thereafter, I received some devastating news. One of the managers of that West Coast company, became enamored by a young lady who worked for a competitive brokerage firm. Needless to say, we immediately lost our biggest line. What was I going to do? How can I let my new employee go?

For the next couple hours, I had for myself what is known as a pity party. To add insult to injury, my cell phone battery malfunctioned and would not take a charge. Still feeling sorry for myself, I drove to a local mall to have my cell phone repaired. While waiting, I bought a cup of coffee and strolled over to the in-door ice rink to watch the children skate. Suddenly, from behind me, I heard a noise unlike anything I had heard before. It sounded to me like an agonizing howl. Turning around, I noticed an elderly woman pushing a young man approx-imately twelve years old in a wheelchair. He wasn't howling or crying; he had a huge smile on his face and that noise was to him laughter. He was clapping and rocking back-and-forth. It occurred to me, that young man would give anything to be able to skate across that rink one time. With tears in my eyes, I forgot all my problems and felt like the most selfish individ-ual on earth. At that moment I repented and asked God to forgive me.

On my drive home I couldn't get that young man out of my mind. As I walked into the office, my wife said, you have a call on line four. When I picked up the phone, the person on the other end said, "Hello Dan, this is Pat from Gloucester, Massachusetts, and I heard you lost your seafood line, and I was wondering if you would be interested in representing our company. It pays approximately $47,000 per year. Needless to say, I was in shock. God chastised me, then forgave me and arranged a $5000 raise. In three short hours, my life went from good, to bad, to better. All because God had it all under control.

*****

For the next few years, my life was somewhat uneventful. I felt God saved me twice because my work here on earth was not yet complete. I attended Moody Bible Institute at the age of 62 and was ordained as a Southern Baptist pastor at 65. For the next 10 years, I kept busy as a jail and prison chaplain along with volunteering at local homeless shelters and holding church services at the local county jail. God showed up twice in a dramatic way, and I was determined to show up for whatever plans he had for me. I was enjoying the peace that God promised, no more drama. However, God wasn't finished testing me.

March 9, 2007, on my birthday, my beautiful daughter Lisa lost her battle with an inoperable brain tumor. For two and a half years Lisa suffered but never once complained as she cast all her cares on the Lord. She prayed constantly,

not for herself, but for her three young children who would be left behind. Three weeks
before her death, she was comatose. In her final hour, hospice, along with her mother and a
few friends gathered around her bed. Suddenly,
Lisa opened her eyes. With a radiant smile
she gazed at an open doorway and exclaimed,
"you've come to get me." Nobody knows what
Lisa saw as they stood speechless. At that moment my little girl laid back with an expression
of serenity and breathed her last. God stepped
in and Lisa was at peace. The Bible says, "no
eye has seen, no ear has heard, no mind can
conceive what God has prepared for those who
love him. (1 Corinthians 2:9) I take great joy in
knowing that Lisa has seen, has heard, and is
enjoying what God had prepared for her.

****

It was a beautiful Florida day on May 13,
2016. I was taking my daily three-mile walk
and rehearsing in my mind a sermon I was
scheduled to give at a local church the following Sunday. The traffic was very sparse in this
golf course community. I saw a few people walking but for the most part I was alone with my
thoughts. Near the end of my walk, I entered a
boardwalk that took me through a wooded area

beside a beautiful lake. I marveled at the exotic birds that inhabited the area which is actually a bird sanctuary. Feeling unusually euphoric, without a care in the world, I continued walking the last five minutes of my daily walk. I stopped, looking both ways before crossing the road toward my home. I was halfway across when my world suddenly went black and I fell backwards in the middle-of-the-road. I had suffered what the doctors referred to as a sudden-death heart attack; no heartbeat, no breath. I was told later by my doctor that I would've had about three minutes to get oxygen to my brain or I would have died.

The following is what the witnesses told my wife. Out of the gated community came one car as I lay motionless on the ground. Miraculously, in that car was a medical doctor. As her husband dialed 911, she immediately began CPR. A few seconds later another car came down the road and stopped when it reached the spot and the driver jumped out to help. She also was a medical doctor. She immediately started checking my pulse as CPR continued. I was told that they were fast wearing out and the rescue vehicle had not yet arrived. By this time there were people everywhere and both sides of the road were closed.

It gets better folks, suddenly a lady came running up to the scene announcing that she was a CPR instructor. All this took place within a short period of time. With massive road construction in our area, it would take an ambulance longer than usual to arrive. Again, the story gets better. The 911 operator announced that there was a full crew across the road not 500 yards away picking up supplies at the supermarket. They arrived within minutes. Twice the paramedics used the defibrillator while speeding to the hospital. The breathing tube was supplying my body with oxygen but the problem was my heart would not continue beating. Three more times in the ER the defibrillator was used and on the third time my heart continued to beat. As my wife and friends arrived at the hospital, they were told I had a 50-50 chance of survival. I spent the next thirty-three days in the hospital and underwent quadruple bypass surgery.

I'm back to living my peaceful life still wondering what God has planned for whatever time I have left on this side of eternity. I often think of the consequences had my heart attack happened a few minutes earlier while in the wooded area out of sight from the road, or thirty seconds later when the three medical professionals would have been gone. I shudder to think about it, and constantly remind myself of Psalm 46:10 : "Be still, and know that I am God."

As I discussed these life experiences with my friends, many of them came forward with wonderful testimonies of their own. The following is a compilation of those spiritual encounters. I pray that you will be blessed while reading the miraculous stories of how God participates in our lives.

Brian N

Romans 8:28 *"And we know that for those who love God, all things work together for good, for those who are called according to his purpose"*

In February of 1992, life seemed to be coming together for me. I was 32 years old, had a regular job, was in a happy relationship, and I also trained candidates for professional wrestling on the side. At 6'2" and 240 pounds, I was an imposing figure when I walked in the room. I had managed to save $91k, and was searching the market for the perfect home in Raleigh, NC. That all came to a screeching halt late one night on a rural highway. I was traveling back home from a wrestling event in Fayetteville, NC, when an impatient driver suddenly darted in my lane from out of a line of traffic heading the opposite way. I had no time to react before contact. The left side of my face was crushed, my shoulder was dislocated, and I suffered serious injuries to my back. The nineteen-year-old driver that hit me wasn't quite as lucky. He died at the scene. Rescue workers were surprised that I survived, and commented that the size of my 1989 Lincoln Town Car probably figured into my survival.

It took me six months of rehabilitation to get back on my feet. By that time, I had lost my job, what I thought was the perfect relationship had ended, and I faced the harsh reality that the other driver had been uninsured, and his family had no money. The financial burden fell almost completely on me, and my insurance. The doctor finally gave me the greenlight to seek employment, and I was able to secure a part time job in the men's department at Belk's Department Store. During Christmas time in 1992, I got sick with what I thought was the flu. I was in my apartment alone when I suddenly found it impossible to breathe. I crawled from the couch, too weak to walk, and managed to get in touch with my neighbor, who drove me to the hospital emergency room. Unable to breathe, I felt life leaving my body as I laid on the gurney. My spirit traveled down a dark tunnel with a blinding light at the end. I could hear my first wife, and other loved ones who had passed before me, calling my name. Suddenly, I was sucked backward as the doctors restarted my heart. I looked upward as my spirit apparition dropped from the ceiling, and reentered my body. The impact left me sore for days afterward. It was determined that I had triple pneumonia, and had been drowning in my own fluids. Once again, my life was spared.

It took me quite a while to get back on my feet. But by then, I was getting into my mid 30's, and had little left of what I once had. I took a job as a trainer at a gym, and worked several other part time jobs to make ends meet. When I looked in the mirror, I saw little of the man I used to be. The accident had left me with hunched shoulders, and the left side of my face drooped with partial permanent nerve damage. Women no longer found me attractive, and I became somewhat of a loner. As if things couldn't get worse, I discovered a lump on one of my testicles in September of 1994. It was determined that it had spread quickly to my lungs and lymph nodes, and was at stage 4, which was pretty much a sure death sentence. The night before my cancer surgery, I was scared, and couldn't sleep. I glanced to the door of my hospital room, and saw a huge black man with enormous muscles standing there with his massive arms crossed in front of him. I asked what he wanted, and he stepped into the light, revealing the most benevolent smile I had ever seen. He answered that he was assigned to watch over me, and that things were going to be alright. I rolled over, and fell into a peaceful sleep. The next morning when the nurses came in to prep me, I asked where the big black guy was that was on duty the night before. They looked at each other rather puzzled, and said that there was no one on that floor that fit that description. To this day, I believe that man was an angel.

For the next three months, I endured some of the harshest chemotherapy, and radiation treatments imaginable. I shrunk down to 165 pounds, lost all my body hair, fingernails, and toe nails. I was so sick, that I actually wanted to die. Shortly after Thanksgiving, my first rounds of treatment had ended, and the doctor called me into her office. I could tell by the look on her face, it was not good news. The chest x-ray had shown that the lungs still carried quite a few cancer cells. She gave me orders to get a cat scan the next day, just so that she could see how much the cancer may have spread. She warned however, that it would be best if I got my final arrangements in order. I went home, and fell to my knees. I asked God that if it was time for me to go, I was willing to accept it. I also asked that if there were any reason for me to live, to please grant me that opportunity to survive. The next day, I went in for the cat scan. The attendant came out when it was done, and said that something had gone wrong, and that she needed to do it again. That was a Friday, and on Monday morning, my doctor called me early and said she needed to see me ASAP. When I walked in her office, she looked at me dumb founded, and held up my file. She said she wasn't a believer, but that something miraculous had taken place. The cat scan was taken twice, and both showed absolutely no sign of cancer in my body. Almost twenty-six years later, she still calls me from time to time, and refers to me as her miracle patient. Once again, God had spared me.

I won't say that life was easy thereafter. I was bankrupt, and basically starting over in my mid 30's. It also took several years for my body to come back from the ordeal. I helped it along by keeping a strict fitness schedule, and a wholistic diet. I took a job at FedEx, where I remained for the next 21 years. In 2009, at the age of 50, I met my present wife. At that point, I had pretty much given up on relationships, and figured I'd be a bachelor for the rest of my life. Our relationship wasn't exactly easy either. She had been abused in her previous relationship. I attended counseling sessions with her, and did everything I could to help her regain her self-esteem. It paid off big. She now has a great job with an accounting firm that pays six figures a year. She had a six-year-old daughter who was shy, and very withdrawn. I realized she had a talent for music, and coached her along over the next several years. She became an accomplished concert pianist, and also learned guitar, and flute. Today she is a student at the University of Buffalo with a full scholar-ship in music. She is also an alternate for the Buffalo Philharmonic. I retired from FedEx in 2017, and am now a successful Screenwriter and Novelist.

As I look back, much good came out of those difficult times. My father and I had always had a rocky relationship. After I was cured of cancer, we became the best of friends. He also rededicated his life to God, and got up every morning for the rest of his life to attend 6AM

Mass at his church. Several of my friends also told me that their faith had been renewed by my ordeal. When my mother became ill with Alzheimer, I was there for her when she had no one else. I realize now that God spared my life because I had a purpose to fulfill, and I certainly hope he's not finished with me yet.

Warren A

*Ephesians 2: 8-9 "For by grace you
have been saved through faith. And
this is not your own doing; it is the gift
of God, not a result of works, so that
no one may boast.*

Life was hard in the thirties and forties especially under the hand of an irresponsible father
who rambled from place to place leaving me
with kinfolk. At the age of eleven he hired me
out to work summers, twelve-hour days, six
days a week. The seventy-two hours earned
me twenty-five dollars which my father appro-
priated. Tiring of constantly pulling him out
of bars in El Paso, I planned to escape. He
threatened to kill me if I didn't accompany him
working construction jobs back east. For two
more years I saw enough construction work in
the booming 1950s to last a lifetime.

He finally split for good in 1952; where to? I
didn't know; nor did I care. I lived in a series

of flop houses until I was fortunate enough to land a job in Chicago earning a decent wage in 1953. I was very lost and confused, to say the least, until a beautiful girl was fooled into marrying me. For that, I thank God daily. If not for my wife, who was and is a strong, devoted Christian wife and mother, I would most likely be dead or dead drunk like my alcoholic father.

After joining the Marine Corp our marriage could still be described as chaotic. As children came along, I had no idea how to be a man, husband or father. We were living hand-to-mouth, paycheck-to-paycheck. Vietnam was heating up and I was sent into combat in 1964, leaving my wife and three children to make it the best they could while I was gone. This separation and combat turned out to be a blessing. My full paycheck was sent home to support my family.

Vietnam was no picnic. One particular day during compact I experienced sheer terror unlike anything I had known at that point. I said a one word, very sincere prayer. H E L P! At that point a ray of light flashed above me. Today one might call it a laser, but the only thing this ray of light illuminated was my heart. I could see it. I still see it today. I began to acknowledge the truth about myself. It's me; I'm a liar, hater, cheater, violent, and bitter person. The list went on and on as I confessed my sins and evil wickedness. I didn't realize, until years later, it was at that moment that I was saved by Yeshua Messiah. I made it out of Vietnam.

Fast forward 15 years. After several years under the tutelage of a wonderful chaplain and then a fiery pastor, my life, marriage, and family of four children began to look up. Unexpectantly, one Fourth of July as we went to visit my wife's widowed mother, my wife approached me and out of the blue, said, "You must go find your father."

"What! What are you talking about? I haven't heard from him in years, he's probably dead."

Her answer to me was, "He must be alive, because God spoke to me that you need to go find your dad."

That was on Wednesday and I had to be back on duty the following Monday. Where do I begin? How do I find someone whose last known address I didn't know? I remembered someone saying years ago that my father had moved to Tampa. That was very long ago. Then, I remembered an old sergeant friend of mine lived in Orlando. I called my old buddy that night and told him I needed to see him the next day. On

Thursday, July 5th, I flew to Orlando. My old friend and I had been involved in many evangelical outreaches so when I told him my problem that I needed to find my father; he had an immediate suggestion. He suggested I start at the last place I heard where he might be.

I answered, "What kind of plan is this?"

"Well," my friend said, "you've got a better plan?"

So, Friday, July 6th, I took his old blue Chevy and drove west to Tampa and began looking through what was known as the skid row area. The street name escapes me now, but I drove up and down that deserted avenue. I came to a very run-down low rent area off the avenue and I felt a nudge. I turned down that side street and spotted a skinny old man. I stopped the car, hoping that if I mentioned my dad's name, he might know him. I rolled my window down, it was a hot, hot Tampa afternoon. This skinny old man looked somewhat familiar. Could this be my dad? Except the last time I had seen my alcoholic father, he was big and round as a barrel, while this old man was skinny. He hobbled up to my car. When he looked me in the face, he stuck his hand through the window and said in a shaky voice, "Son, I think it's time

I met Jesus." Gone was the callused hand of a hardened construction worker. That day July 6, 1979, my father confessed his sins and evil wickedness and was saved by Yeshua Messiah. His own personal battle of sixty-five years had come to a glorious end. What a miracle! What are the odds; three million people in the Tampa Bay Area and the first person I saw was my long lost flesh and blood!

The miraculous events that led to my father's salvation began another battle within me. I began to re-live all my sins. I remembered how I had suffered at his hand and how he had enslaved me. How I blamed him for my troubled life, marriage and family problems. On the flight home, God spoke to me personally, not through my wife, or my old sergeant friend; this time, he spoke to me personally. How many sins can you attribute to your father, he asked; sins which you blamed him for your own troubled life? Well, God, there must be at least 100 maybe 200. That still small voice answered. If you can see 200 sins of your father with your eyes of flesh, how many sins do you believe I see in you with my eye of spirit?

Yahweh's revelation terrified me. I could finally see the tally sheet with zero after zero; the

200, 2000, or 20,000. It suddenly occurred to me that I am the worst sinner I know. A passage from the Bible came to me at that moment. (Matthew 7:3) *"why do you look at the speck in your brother's eye, but fail to notice the log in your own."*

Wade W

Psalm 143:8 "Let me hear in the morning of your steadfast love, for in you I trust. Make me know the way I should go, for to you I lift up my soul."

I grew up in what might be considered a dysfunctional home. My father was a biker and an alcoholic. He ruled with an iron fist and eventually my parents were divorced. I felt very much alone growing up. In first and second grade I attended a catholic school; then after that I was pretty much a heathen until I was 38 years old. At the age of 13 I discovered my talent and passion was music and began playing the guitar and singing. When I was 16, I played in a heavy metal band and cut my first record while touring. The band was successful and everything was paid for. At first, I only began drinking alcoholic beverages; then the life style led me to drugs. Most kids from broken homes tend to blame their parents. As I grew older and defeated drugs and alcohol, I came to understand that my dad did what he could with what he was given.

I perform on the weekends at a restaurant in Sanford, FL and that weekend, January 16, 2016, started out as a fairly normal day. I woke up not feeling well. Nothing I could put my finger on; just feeling out of sorts. But I knew I had to go and do the gig in Sanford. Even though it was a two-hour drive, as truth be told, I really needed the money.

I was into my third set when the manager, Larry, told me I could finish and pack up and forget about doing a fourth set. He said he would pay me what they owned me and I could just go home. The restaurant wasn't very busy so I started to breakdown my equipment. I was carrying some of my equipment out when he came back to me said he changed his mind and really would like to hear some more music. He had never done this before and I thought it to be rather strange, but thinking of the money, I said, "okay". So, I carried my guitar case back in and started to play the fourth set.

At the end of the fourth and final set I started to feel extremely bad. I had been singing for four hours and my headache was getting worse.

While loading all my equipment in the car which was parked in the front of the restaurant, I completely lost all ability to move and dropped to the ground unable to move my arms and legs. This happened for a split second and then it was gone. That was unlike anything I've experienced in my entire life. In that moment I chalked it off as being overly tired. So, I went back into the restaurant to say goodbye to everyone which I usually do to thank the people. By this time the pain in my head was excruciating; it felt like someone was hitting the back of my head with a sledge hammer. I asked if anyone had Tylenol or something else, I could take. While drinking some liquid, my headache was so bad that I barely could see and asked for a bag of ice to put on the back of my neck. The next thing I was aware of, I had dropped to the floor and I could not move again; paralyzed. I didn't know what was happening to me. Could I have been poisoned by something? Thoughts raced through my mind. Next, I felt some fingers on my wrist and a voice saying, "he has no pulse!" I was faintly aware of screaming around me, and I began to feel some compressions on my chest and then the world went black.

To finish this part of the story, I awoke in the

Emergency Room, hearing someone say, "you need to sign this form authorizing surgery or you're going to die." Evidently, I had a brain aneurysm rupture. I blanked out again, woke up briefly in a helicopter and six weeks later awoke from a coma. In the space of six weeks, I had lived through two brain operations. Once awake I was told I had to go into weeks of therapy in a facility to learn to move, walk and speak again. I couldn't swallow, although I could barely utter out a few words. Then God gave me a second miracle. Within four or five days after my second brain surgery, I was able to walk to a wheel chair. At that point, I insisted on going home. In six months, I learned to walk, talk and become totally self -sufficient.

What was my first miracle? The first miracle was who God placed at that restaurant to save my life. Who were these people? Two sisters and a best friend from Kansas City, Missouri. Their husbands had been invited to a well-known fishing tournament in Sanford at the last minute. They decided to take the opportunity bringing along their wives to enjoy a quick get-a-way weekend. All the hotels were booked but they managed to get the last room, which they all had to share, at a small hotel right next to the restaurant where I played.

They were at the bar and were about to leave and return to their room because they wanted to see the Kansas City Chiefs game on T.V. and the bar didn't have it on. As they were leaving, Larry offered to put the game on without sound since I was still playing my music. Music that I shouldn't have been playing. I didn't want to do the show that day but because I needed the money, I was there. To this day, I shudder to imagine how many lives may have been lost on Interstate 4 heading back to Tampa if Larry had not called me back to finish playing out the fourth set. I would have crashed. Who or what would I have hit when I blanked out? Would several innocent people have lost their lives? One thing is certain, I wouldn't have survived.

The person whose fingers I felt taking my pulse turned out to be emergency room nurses, wives of the fishing buddies; experienced medical persons whom God placed there. They should have been home in Kansas City, but they were at the only hotel available next to the restaurant. Even the fact that Larry was nudged by something to have me play a fourth set. Was that the Holy Spirit? All these things had to work in perfect order for me to survive that day.

Twice I was brought back to life with them performing chest compressions. While they must have felt the rush of adrenaline, I felt strange, like I was out of my body, completely at peace; void of anything else. A very beautiful feeling of total acceptance of being dead entered my mind. I'm dead, I'm going to Heaven and I'm okay with it. I was completely surprised of the acceptance of that. I couldn't change anything so I was okay with it. Memories were there, but no panic, just acceptance. It felt like forever to me, but the nurses told me it was only four to five minutes. You really don't know. I was waiting for Christ to come to take me to heaven. If God had given me a choice, I would have gone with him. I was okay with moving ahead in God's kingdom if He had allowed that. But it wasn't my choice to make. Why did God spare me?

It occurred to me after I was fully recovered and back to living my life, that we humans have no idea of the amazing web of God's movement all over the world. I see that God's plan is tailor-made for me. In my early years, in the midst of living in an excess of drugs and alcohol, I came to the time that something had to change in my life. I met an amazing person who had an incredible influence on my life. Although he hung around with the same group of musicians at parties, there was something different about him. He was successful and amazingly good looking, but he never judged those around him and what they were doing, I said to him in all my circle of friends, you seem to have it all together. What is your secret? He looked me in the eyes and said, "my relationship with Jesus Christ." His answer stunned me, but got me thinking, I need what he has. One evening I got on my knees and asked Jesus Christ to come into my life, to come into my heart and make me the man he wanted me to be. Not a different person but the person I was created to be. Life has never been better since that day.

God gave me a glimpse of Heaven outside my body. I'm not trying to second guess God, but I believe that He spared me so I could see this amazing fact of keeping one musician alive, I'm given the opportunity to share the Gospel of Jesus Christ. I'm able to share my story of hope and miracles. These miracles proved to me that the material things of this world do not matter. It is the peace and joy we can find in each other and in the saving Grace of God.

Today, I'm an actor making commercials, a musician, and a husband. Not having seen Jesus while I was in that void, caused me to question my faith. But even not seeing him, I would have chosen to stay in that peaceful state. I really wanted to see God. I felt completely alone. I have battled demons my entire life as a seeker of pleasure, but alone in that void I felt complete love. The pleasures of this world for me, becoming rich and famous, acting awards, are still important but it doesn't matter what people think of me. What matters is I really want God's approval because now I know what lies beyond this life. What we see as important now doesn't matter in the end. I want to help direct people to understand there is a loving creator guiding and loving all of us. Whether I'm famous or have a job working at McDonalds, if I'm living for Christ, the end result is the same.

May God Bless you all and may the reading of my miracles help you to find true peace with God.

Lizzy M

Psalm 16:8 *"I have set the Lord always before me; because he is at my right hand, I shall not be shaken."*

The morning came as any other; however, my stomach knew this was not just another day. It was time to initiate my plan. I spent my free time gathering minor items that were needed to gain my freedom. In the weeks prior, I found a small box for my things that was easy to carry. Time was of the essence, and there was no room for error. Since evening was setting in, I had to complete my chores and prepare for the escape. On the backside of the house, we had a small planter that I stashed my box out of sight. My mind focused on the idea of finally being free, I only had to survive one more night.

As the afternoon faded, my stomach churned, but I had to keep focused on the mission at hand. In a way, I already felt free. For the first time, the extent of the beatings was of no concern to me tonight. My only thoughts were about getting out alive.

I heard the back door open and my husband come inside; he called my name, then asked if his dinner was ready. I calmly replied it was finished on the table and explained I had already eaten and was not hungry. Of course, my statement set him off, as usual, then right on cue, I heard the plate shatter across the tile floor. My usual nightmare ensured.... I found myself curled up on the floor in a fetal position to protect my body from the blows. As he continued to thrash, I lay, wondering how long the beating would last this time. The only survival mechanism I had to endure this chaos was to leave my body and stop all conscious thought and feeling. As I had learned long ago, falling into my trance served me well, tonight especially.

If my husband followed suit, once his ranting started, the brutality stopped immediately. He'd walk out of the room, shouting, laughing at the pathetic sight he saw lying on the floor, then barked demands as he disappeared down the hallway. As time passed, trying to regain my composure got more difficult by the minute. Sometimes, I had to crawl until I was strong enough to stand. It was easier to avoid the pain by just staying on the floor, however, that night I knew freedom lay just beyond the door.

Once I managed to stand, it was imperative to stay silent. On most nights, he would fall asleep shortly after the beatings stopped when he laid on the couch. So, I waited until darkness took over the sky, and his snoring rattled the house. I tipped-toed out of the bathroom, through the living room, and headed to the backdoor. My purse was sitting on the chest freezer in the laundry room. My earlier apprehensions left quickly; the concept of freedom seeped into my soul.

My friend was waiting down the street, a clear distance from my house. But I had no reason to hurry, she'd wait all night if necessary. The only priority that mattered was getting out alive. When I reached for the door handle, my first taste of freedom was soothing and brought a complete sense of peace over my body. I turned and gently closed the backdoor, moving across the patio to grab my box from the planter. The further I got from the house a sensation came over my body, that I had never felt before. My nightmare was truly ending, this time I woke alive and unharmed.

The local women's shelter was not far, and my friend was happy to see me alive. The shelter was not home or where I wanted to spend my time, but it was a start. The attendant assigned me a cot and dresser drawer for my belongings. I slowly took the items out of the box and laid them one by one on the cot. But as I looked at the items, I realized the horror endured for so many years left me with nothing but broken bones and terrifying nightmares. My life had no meaning; in fact, I had no life at all. In essence, the time spent enduring the abuse was in vain, because it left nothing but a veil of dark experiences. Reality reared its ugly head, and I saw the truth. I knew there had to be a better way to live. No matter how hard this seemed at the moment, nothing could resemble my experiences.

After scanning each of my items and laying them neatly in the drawer, I looked around the shelter. Across the room, a woman was sitting on the edge of a cot, and a sense of urgency came over my soul. The energy carried me to her side. We sat in silence for some time before she spoke. I held her in my arms, hoping to calm the terror she felt inside. Nonetheless, as the night wore on, fear overtook her and she fell into a trance. A look I had seen many times on my own face. In the moment, a song formed in my head and I sang gallantly most of the night, trying to calm both myself and her troubled heart. By morning's light, she had survived her first night of freedom. However, the daylight only added additional concerns. As she regained consciousness, the worry overtook any rational decision making.

She began exclaiming, "I have to leave, this was a mistake. He has calmed down now, I'll be alright. I will just tell him I went for a walk."

The fear she felt was overwhelming, and I pleaded with her over and over, "You are not invisible out there, please don't leave. Please don't leave, it's not safe yet."

Later that day, I was forced to leave myself, but I begged her to stay, "Give it more time, please don't leave," I told her.

"I'll be alright. . . . Thank you for everything. I promise to stay." Her words eased my fears.

As I headed for the door, the wrenching pain in my stomach grew rapidly. It forced me to turn back and see her face one more time as I left the shelter. The sheer terror harbored inside her eyes bore clear through my soul. It was a look I would never forget. Uncertain of my own fate, I knew the risks of leaving the shelter, but important business took me outside safety. When I returned later that afternoon, I immediately looked for her and saw the cot had been assigned to someone else. The staff reported she left soon after I had. They could not convince her to stay.

My heart sank, knowing the terror she would face. Nothing could shake the look I saw in her eyes earlier that day. The next several hours were almost unbearable. All the pain, anguish, and sorrow I felt rushed over of me like a broken dam. There are no words to describe the feelings running through my head.

Later that night her cot was re-assigned to another woman, leaving all the beds full once again. However, tonight the shelter was empty for me. I slipped into my trance and fell asleep, curled up in a ball, sobbing from the pain. As the sun rose the next morning, the rays warmed my face. I looked around and heard nothing, it was a peaceful, serene setting and freedom took over my soul.

Then God stepped in; the moment had come for me to understand my true calling in life. Many years have passed since that day, but none go by without seeing her face and the intensity of the pain that plagued her soul. I can still hear her say, "It's alright, I'll be okay. He's calmed now. It's alright, I'll be okay."

Those were the defining words that brought light to the realities of domestic abuse.   I promised myself that morning to do whatever it took to find a safe passage for women seeking a way out. In that commitment, I created the Purposed Survivor 12-Step program. Her death will forever plague my soul, and for that reason, this story needed to be told.

God does not always step in for the reason we think, but he never fails to protect those who suffer for an unyielding pain they can no longer endure. It is because of these women who died from an abusive situation that this program was formed.

Please always give a moment of silence for the individuals who still suffer in domestic abuse situations. Pray for their souls and the path that leads to freedom. The story was not meant to deter you from becoming a Purposed Survivor, but to ensure your understanding of the violent realities that are intertwined with domestic abuse.

Don H

Ephesians 6:10 *"Finally, be strong in the Lord and in the strength of his might."*

In 1998, I began working a volunteer position for an international ministry that worked with Christians around the world who were suffering for their faith. In 1999 and 2000, my wife Brenda and I smuggled Bibles into Vietnam, Laos, and Iran. One of the nations in which the ministry was very involved was the war-torn region of Sudan, which is now South Sudan as they've separated into their own nation. It was in South Sudan where we witnessed the most heart-breaking situation of orphaned children caused by the fleeing and massacre of thousands. Brenda and I were simultaneously led by God to take on what seemed an impossible mission. The mission was to adopt some of these helpless children. I remember saying to God, "All right; I'll do this. But you have to do the heavy lifting. I have nothing to bring to the table except for obedience." **Genesis 27:8 *"Now, therefore, my son, obey my voice as I command you."***

We began by speaking with a man from the ministry who had made several trips there and had spent a great deal of time ministering in the region. When we explained to him our intentions, his answer was, "if it was possible to bring children from South Sudan to the United States, I would already have had a house full; it simply isn't possible." The explanation was that the Muslim Sudanese government in control was the entity doing the violence which caused the children to be orphaned in the first place. Many of them had fled to refugee camps in Kenya, but we couldn't adopt them from Kenya since the children weren't Kenyans. We couldn't adopt them from the United Nations, because the UN doesn't get involved. Our response to him was, ***"with man this is impossible, but with God all things are possible."*** **Matthew 19:26.**

Soon after, we were told of a man in California who had actually managed to do it, not once, but twice. We contacted him and he was willing to help us explaining everything he had done and got us in contact with his Kenyan attorney. I called the attorney who assured us that we would be able to do this. We were also given the contact information of a Catholic nun who had been helping thousands of Sudanese orphans for decades. She assured us that she had many orphans in need of parents. The attorney told me to come to Kenya so I could identify the orphans and she was prepared to do the necessary paperwork. I would need to stay there for two months, which was no problem.

In America, we needed to be approved as adoptive parents by our government. The woman asked us how many children we were interested in adopting, but we had no idea. God had said, "Go get children." He hadn't mentioned a number. Our thinking was a boy and a girl sounded about right. Not wanting to assume God's intention, we didn't indicate a number. We asked the woman how many children would we be approved to adopt? Thus, when I left for Kenya, I was anticipating maybe a total of five children.

Once we began taking the actions of actually doing this, God began doing the "heavy lifting." We had been renting a house for the past seven years. It was just barely large enough for me,

Brenda and our three biological children. We had always been interested in buying a home of our own, but were never able to save any money towards making that a possibility. Again, God stepped in.

On 9/11/01 (Yep, that infamous day!) a realtor called us about a house which would meet our needs. We immediately looked at it and decided that it would be right for us. We were approved for a VA loan which required no down payment but did require an inspection. The sellers agreed to pay all closing costs if we paid their asking price. When the realtor found out which inspector had been assigned to the house, we were informed this could present a major hurdle in that this particular inspector was very strict and would probably not pass it." However, he instructed us to make some minor changes including some roof repairs. The sellers agreed to pay the roof repairs at closing. Less than two months after first setting eyes on the house, we moved in. We hadn't had to pay a penny to accomplish that and we got a check to cover the cost of the roof repairs.

Already being a family of five, and looking to increase that number, we were going to need a larger vehicle. God stepped in again. We were given an eight-passenger van by a man whom we have, to this day, never met. Another man donated $3,000 dollars towards the adoption expenses.

To add to our trials, I was involved in a work place accident requiring four surgeries. What the enemy meant for evil, God turned to good. I was unable to work for two years which gave me the time to deal with the volume of clerical and legal issues. Like Joseph said in **Genesis 50:20** *"As for you, you meant evil against me, but God meant it for good."*

When I arrived in Kenya, I went to the attorney's office. When I met her, she asked, "Why are you here?" She then told me that, even if it were going to be possible to adopt Sudanese children through the Kenyan government, Kenya law dictated that all prospective adoptive parents must have the children live in their home with them for a minimum of six months as a "trial period." Even though the job seemed insurmountable, I then went to see the Catholic nun. When I first met the nun, she had a toddler and a young (about 11) boy with her. The boy was helping her with whatever she needed, including changing toddler diapers. The nun had five siblings, three of which were

too old to be adopted, so she was recommend-
ing that we adopt the youngest two (a boy and
a girl), which I agreed to. The next day, I was
told that the boy asked the nun why I didn't
want to adopt him, too. Perhaps he was too old.
I simply hadn't even thought of it. Brenda and
I had personally been thinking of a boy and a
girl, and that's what was presented to me. I
called Brenda (who had already been informed
about the two siblings) and told her of the boy.
She immediately agreed, and so now we were
on our way to adopting three children, two boys
12 and 6, and a girl of 10.

Throughout our process, everything that was
"easy" was impossible, and everything that was
"impossible" was easy. In order to adopt the
children, we needed their birth certificates and
the death certificates of their parents. For the
death certificates, I simply typed up forms with
the information as well as we knew it. Amazingly, that was totally acceptable for everyone
involved. The children's UN paperwork had
their ages listed, but no birthdates, so we simply made them up. The youngest child's birthday was actually made to be the last day that
he would still be the age that was on his form.
The oldest child had been given a "birthday" by

the nun. When he told us what that was, we misunderstood him. One of the very last things we had to do was to sit down with an official from the embassy just to make certain that the children on the paperwork were real. When he mentioned the birthdate, it was about a week off. The official told our son that it would be easier if he just kept the birthdate that was on the form, so he got a new birthday that day.

We had been put in touch with one of the most highly respected members of parliament in the Kenyan government who was very willing to help us as well as a U.S. Senator. We believed that these high-level individuals would be an asset to our cause. We soon learned that the exact opposite was true. Due to politics even mentioning those people caused immediate anger and resentment with the local officials and bureaucrats we needed to work with.

We finally found that the only way to accomplish this was to seek guardianship of the children rather than seeking adoption which is what we did. This would allow us to bring them home. Once we had them in the U.S., we could adopt them through the standard American government system... We were finally all ready with our paperwork and approvals and ready to come home. A day before we were to leave Kenya, we were informed that we would not be allowed to fly via Amsterdam because the Netherlands had been having problems with child trafficking. People were "adopting" children, but when they landed in Amsterdam, supposedly just a transit point, the children would disappear into sex slavery or even organ harvesting.

We literally ran all over Nairobi, trying to get our KLM tickets changed to British Air. We went to the Dutch embassy and were miraculously able to get them to give us travel visas for the children accomplished in a single day. We successfully flew to Amsterdam where we had a 24-hour layover. We were not allowed to leave the transit area of the airport, but we were able to get a small hotel room for eight hours to get some sleep.

When we landed in Detroit, we had just a forty-five-minute layover, but were held up at immigration because they told us that the children's visas were not sufficient to allow them into the country. Their "visas" were one-inch thick, sealed manilla envelopes stuffed with every form we had accumulated over the past two months. It was looking like we were stuck for good. We couldn't bring them into the United States, but we certainly couldn't turn around and go back to Africa.

At this point we looked at each in a feeling of helplessness. Then the woman said, "If only you had UN paperwork for them." Miraculously, we had that and handed over their UNHCR refugee forms. Even then, I didn't have much hope that these would be helpful. One was expired and the other was over two years old and didn't even have the child's picture on it since he had fled South Sudan with his uncle. What we had was a copy of the uncle's form, with his picture. The only thing connecting it to our child was that his name was one of eight who had travelled with the uncle.

Fortunately, the American officials were delighted with the forms, spent ten grueling minutes crafting (think scissors, tape and glue) more official visas for the children. We were allowed to continue on to our home with the children managing to just barely catch our flight.

In the end, God's hand was evident throughout the process. I had told God that we brought nothing to the table except for a willingness to obey. Even then, my ego figured that I had a few tricks up my sleeve. We had the example and assistance of the man who had done it before; that turned out to be worthless. Our process was different from his in every way. We had the willingness of highly respected officials from both America and Kenya, but that "help" nearly ruined everything for us. God allowed us to try using our "strengths" to get this done. But, at every point, we realized that we had absolutely nothing. The instant we came to that realization (often with a lot of weeping), God graciously accomplished what we had been working on, but in an entirely different way than we had even imagined. We had government officials and people who had done it. God used work-place injuries, expired forms and pieces of paper typed up in lieu of official certificates. "But HE showed to me, "My grace is sufficient for you, for MY power is made perfect in weakness." Therefore, I will boast all the more gladly about my weaknesses, so that Christ's power may rest on me. That is why, for Christ's sake, I delight in weaknesses, in insults, in hardships, in persecutions, in difficulties. For when I am weak, then I am strong." II Cor. 12:9-10

Pastor Steven B

Psalm 34:17 *"When the righteous cry for help, the Lord hears and delivers them out of all their troubles."*

I was a volunteer at our local church on Florida's West Coast back in 2011. As an ordained Pastor, my job was to answer emergency calls to the church during off hours. The emergency number was forwarded to my cell phone 24/7. The majority of calls did not, however, constitute an emergency. They usually consisted of requests for directions to the church or service times.

One Thursday evening while returning from a friend's home, an emergency call came in. I know one should never assume, but with heavy traffic, I decided to wait thirty minutes until I arrived home before calling back the number. I figured if it was important, they would leave a message.

I've often heard people refer to God speaking in a small still voice. In my entire life, I never heard God speak until that night. The voice wasn't audible, but in my mind these words flashed, "Call back now." It was unlike anything I'd ever experienced. I immediately pulled into a strip mall and called the number.

The person was a male whose voice was one of desperation. He asked if I was a pastor. My answer was, "Yes, how can I help you?"

He answered, "I have a question. If someone commits suicide, can he still go to heaven?"

My response was, "Where are you?"

His location was about four miles away. I instructed him to go to a waffle house which was near his location and I'd be wearing a cap with Jesus on the front and I'd be there in fifteen minutes.

The restaurant was nearly empty and I saw him at a table in the far corner. He stood as I approached and I noticed his eyes weld up in tears. For the next two hours, we drank enough coffee to keep an elephant awake for a week, as he spoke and I listened to his story.

He had recently lost his mother to a stroke and shortly after his wife informed him that she was in love with another man and was pregnant with his child. If that wasn't enough, his business was going into bankruptcy. He was driving toward a bridge which is known for suicides. In his most desperate hour, he googled churches near his location and called our emergency number. When I didn't answer his call, he was even more determined to end his life.

Had I waited until I got home, my new friend could possibly have been gone. After talking through all his problems and possible solutions, he began to feel better. Although he hadn't been in a church for many years, we discussed a lot of things he remembered from Sunday school as a child, especially the story of Job.

As we departed, he assured me that suicide was no longer an option. I gave him my personal cell number and he promised to keep in touch. The following Sunday at church, I saw his smiling face as he approached me and gave me a big hug while whispering thank you in my ear.

Shortly thereafter, he was offered a very lucrative job out of state. The last I heard; he surrendered his life to Jesus. He was active in a church in Georgia where he met a sweet woman who was the church worship leader and soon to be his wife.

That small still voice is real.

Jerry D

Psalm 30:2 *"O Lord my God, I cried to you for help, and you have healed me."*

I was born in Toledo, Ohio on January 7, 1947. At the age of six years, I was diagnosed with tuberculosis and not expected to live. I spent a year in the TB hospital in Toledo. As my grandfather was a Free-Will-Baptist Preacher, he had many, many people praying for my recovery. In answer to prayer, finally one year later, I was healed and allowed to return home.

Even though my grandfather was a preacher, I was not raised in a church environment. I did not attend church until I was thirty years old and met my future wife there. At the age of forty, I accepted Christ as my Savior while visiting my brother-in-law's church. Shortly after I accepted Christ, the Lord spoke to my heart and told me that miracles and joys would be with me. At the time, I didn't know what that meant. In the following years, it became clear what miracles and joys I would see.

In the late 80s, I fell on a steel grate at work and injured my knee. However, I did not report this to my supervisor and as time went on the pain in my knee increased dramatically. One day while on my way to work, I told my wife to call the doctor and make an appointment. Walking into the plant that day, the pain was so intense that I raised my hands and called out to Jesus. At that moment a warm feeling came over my knee and, by the time I reached the entrance to the plant, the pain was gone and I was walking fine. I thanked God for granting my prayer!

My second miracle was an outbreak of hives on most of my body which showed as red blotches. This included swelling of my lips and throat. The doctors were afraid of my throat swelling shut, not being able to breathe, so this meant I had to carry medication with me constantly. This medication made me extremely drowsy which in turn made it difficult to work. During this time, my wife and I joined a Sunday night prayer group at church. This group prayed for many things, a new youth pastor, needs of the church and also the prayer request of others, which included prayer for my constant medical condition. I was not healed immediately! Approximately three years later on Palm Sunday, while at church during Praise and Worship, I noticed that the red blotches on my arms had vanished. Praise the Lord I was healed of this awful disease!

In the late 90s, my wife and I had become very active in the church. I was director of missions, training and leading mission trips to other countries. We were planning a mission trip to Venezuela with members of our church. On Sunday there was going to be a meeting with anyone interested in joining our mission team. I got up on Sunday morning and felt like I was coming down with the flu, so I asked her to handle the whole meeting. When she returned home, she found our bedroom door barely hanging. I told her that I had passed out and didn't know what happened. She called our doctor and he told her to take me to the emergency room. By the time we reached the emergency room, I was too weak to get out of the car. An orderly came out and carried me in. They immediately hooked me up to all kinds of equipment. I spent several hours in the emergency room because they were afraid to unhook me from the equipment to move me to a room. When I finally was transferred to a room, I was curled tight in a fetal position and very ill. It was discovered that I had a serious blood infection and the doctors were doubtful I would survive the night. But God had other plans for me. After five days in the hospital, I was healed and released. I was then told that I should not go to Venezuela and to stay out of higher elevations. A few months later I went to Venezuela high in the Andes Mountains Praising the Lord.

At age 55 we joined a worldwide mission's organization, moved to Florida and were directors of two ministries. I am now an Ordained Pastor.

This is not the end of my Miracles and Joys! There are miracles and joys every day.

All Praise Goes to Jesus Christ!!

Paula L

Psalm 130:1-2a *"Out of the depths I cry to You. O Lord. Lord hear my voice!"*

I'm a single mom with two sons and a daughter. I work full time; have many friends and family and I take great joy in my life and my children. On a day in March 2006 my whole world was turned upside down.

My mom was driving on Route 9 in Framingham, Massachusetts with my sister in the car beside her. My 14-year-old son, Richie, and my sister's 2-year-old daughter were sitting in the back seat. They were sitting at a traffic light when my sister noticed that a big box truck was bearing down on them. In a split second she shouted out, "He's not stopping," but it was too late. My son threw himself over the baby while the car rolled over multiple times, landing on the roof. Part of the car was like an accordion. Everyone but my younger son escaped with minor injuries. Richie's injuries were horrific; his brain was exposed and there was damage to his brain stem.

He was airlifted to the hospital where he remained in critical condition. The doctors told us he had a forty percent chance of surviving his injuries. His skull was removed due to extreme swelling; he had a feeding tube, and trach tube for breathing. His right side was totally paralyzed. Once he regained consciousness, he was unable to speak and doctors had determined that he would spend the rest of his life in a wheelchair also unable to walk. Miraculously the cognitive portion of his brain remained functioning and he was able to understand what we were asking of him.

In these long months my mother was my rock. She kept me going when I would get discouraged. I was raised Catholic as a child and my mother at some point had joined a Christian church and as a result, she spent many hours praying for Richie's recovery.

The months after the accident, his 23-year-old brother, Angel, spent as many hours as he could sitting with his brother, encouraging him to recover. They were very close and Richie idolized his older brother. The accident and Richie's condition were devastating to all of us.

I quit work as we lived off my 401K funds that year. Angel was working two jobs and splitting his time between work and the hospital. This put a strain on his serious relationship with his girlfriend who was expecting their first child. They split up and he met a girl on the Myspace app on the Internet.

September 12 started like any other day. We were six months into our hospital and work routine when the unthinkable happened. My son, Angel, Richie's brother, my first born, died of Cardiac pulmonary edema. I didn't believe it. No, it couldn't be. He's only 23! I had kissed him goodbye that morning and told him I loved him. He had gone to a party at the girl's home, the one he met on Myspace. The police arrested her as she was on probation for armed robbery and they found a mixture of alcohol, cocaine and prescription pills. We don't know the details of that night, only that Angel had a combination of uppers, downers and alcohol in his system, and the girl wouldn't disclose what exactly happened.

My days became a living nightmare. The accident, the hospital, the shock of Angel's death, and the funeral. I wanted to die. I questioned, "why is this happening to me? What have I done to deserve this?"

I began to hate God. How could a loving God let this happen?

We didn't tell Richie at first because we were afraid what it would do to him. I sunk into a deep depression and the devil seemed to take over. I was overwhelmed. I felt that everything was too much of an effort. My days seemed to get darker and darker. I was beginning to feel that there was no way I could cope anymore and I started to think about dying. Why not? I felt my life was over. It didn't matter what people said to me, nothing anyone would say could make it any better. No one could take away the pain of my loss.

Day to day my thoughts dwelt more and more on simply ending it all. I was convinced this was my only choice. So, without any deep thought, one day I decided to do it. I'll just go into my basement and hang myself. I started down the stairs when I felt a presence and saw an apparition, a white-robed shadow in human form wearing a gown pass by me. I didn't know why, but I recognized it as a message from God. I heard a voice in my head tell me to go back up the stairs, remember your son needs you. Was that an angel? I only know that something was there. When I was at the depth of depression, God helped me and all thought of committing suicide was over.

My attitude changed after that. I started praying and asked God to forgive me for the hate I had felt towards him. My healing had started.

After spending one year at the Francesca Children's Rehab Hospital, doctors determined that Richie should be moved to a care facility.

I have been raised in a loving family with the belief that family comes first and that we take care of our own. There was no way we were going to send him away. We moved Richie home and he became my full-time responsibility. I didn't want to accept the possibility that he would never walk again. I set up a physical therapy area in the basement and hired a personal trainer to work with him. In the State of Massachusetts, a person can remain in school until 23 years of age. I made sure that he was able to finish his high school. He learned to communicate by some simple sign language. His teachers were wonderful. He graduated and was able to walk slowly with a cane at his high school prom. Although, he needs the wheel chair for longer distance.

Because of the accident, he requires medication to control his depression. Richie spends his time in the gym and using his I-pod for music which he loves. He makes videos on TikTok and has over one million followers! He smiles a lot and is very loving. Although he will never be able to speak or live alone due to his entire right side being paralyzed, his mind is sharp. He still needs 24-hour care and always will. But God spared his life and saved mine.

In 2016 my mom found out she had stage 4 lung cancer. At the time they gave her months to live. She fought for as long as she could after moving in with me and Richie. She was able to live two years longer than was predicted.

My life is not perfect. Being a care-giver is very demanding and is continuous. I still have days when I get lonely and wish my life had been different. But I handle it better because I know God is with me. I don't attend church; I just have conversations with God. I love differently now. I cherish my only grandson, born soon after Angel died. My love overflows day to day because you never know if you will have another day. I pray fervently that God will allow me to have many, many years more so I can take care of Richie.

Rose D

Psalm 120:1 *"In my distress I called to the Lord, And He answered me."*

Psalm 30:2 *"O Lord my God, I cried to you for help, and you have healed me."*

March of 1979 my mom, Kate, was diagnosed with an aggressive breast cancer and given six months to live. Needless-to-say, we were all in shock. Her doctors set her up for a complete mastectomy followed by three series of chemo and radiation therapies. In spite of what was expected, we praised the Lord that my mom never got sick or lost any of her hair during these therapies.

In order to give her the best opportunity to survive the cancer, her doctors offered to try an experimental treatment. She was more than willing to try this treatment. It consisted of the placement of a large plastic clear-like bandage over her surgery area. They left small air-like pockets from which to draw out the poison from her breast area by using a small syringe inserted into air pockets to pull the cancer poison from the "bandage". The treatment proved successful. Our prayers were answered and she was pronounced cancer free.

However, a couple of years later, the cancer did return and so chemo and radiation were started again. But during the radiation treatments, a silver-dollar-size hole was burned into the side of her breast area deep down to her ribs. This did not heal over time. It was determined that a series of two plastic surgeries spaced months apart were needed to close the hole.

The first surgery was completed with no problems. A couple of months later she was scheduled for the second surgery. For whatever reason, my mom was very nervous about this second hospital surgery. The morning she was scheduled to go to the hospital, she asked me if I had heard her scream out during the night. I said, "no, I didn't hear anything." She told me that Jesus had, "come to her," during the night and told her not to worry that he would take care of everything. I took mom to the hospital and her surgery was scheduled the next day.

Mom called me about 6:00 a.m. and said the surgeon had been in and everything looked good for the surgery to start about 9:30 a.m. At about 6:30 my aunt called me and said that I would have company for dinner; she repeated this a couple of times. I finally asked her what she was talking about and she told me my mom was coming home; then she explained what happened.

For some reason the anesthesiologist wanted to talk with my mom, so the anesthesiologist and the surgeon came to see her. When the doctor removed the covering from her wound, they discovered it was completely healed! The surgeon kind of stuttered and stared speechless at what had been a hole, was now a completely healed spot. He said, "I didn't do this!"

As my mom was preparing to leave the hospital, a nurse asked her who she gave credit to for this healing. My mom's answer was "Jesus Christ." She had called out to Jesus for help and he healed her. Over the years we referred many times to mom's three miracles. The first, no sickness or loss of hair. The second miracle was her first healing after the experimental cancer treatment. The third miracle was the peace her mom had experienced when Jesus had come to her and his gift of healing her wound. God had answered our prayers in a miraculous way. After this she lived out her life cancer free for 10 years.

Kyle L

John 4:48 *So Jesus said to him, "unless you see signs and wonders you will not believe."*

While growing up, I only ever saw the inside of a church for weddings and funerals. I never had the desire to get involved with religious things. However, in 1991 after the birth of my son, I felt attending the church would be a good family activity. We could connect with good moral people and my son and daughter would interact with well-disciplined friends. My wife and I enjoyed the coffee and conversation before and after service in the Fellowship Hall. My wife joined the ladies Bible study which resulted in a positive transformation in her. I, on the other hand, was content to be part of a great group of people.

People like me are known as cafeteria Christians; i.e. I'll have a little bit of some things; a lot of others and I don't want anything to

interfere with my worldly pleasures of which
my favorite was socializing with my unsaved
friends at a local watering hole in town. However, most evenings I would sit at home watch-
ing a baseball game while my daughter Carrie
would deliver me a beer whenever I called for
one. I called her my little barmaid. Gradually
my trips to the local bar replaced my drinking
at home. I must admit I also enjoyed flirting
with members of the opposite sex, nothing serious, just good fun. One evening a young
lady named Barbara came on to me in a very
friendly manner. To make a long story short, we
both ended up drinking more than we should
have. She invited me to her apartment for coffee and I immediately accepted the invitation.
We drove my car and I promised to bring her
back for her own vehicle when we were both
capable of driving safely. Needless to say, the
few hours we spent together was more than
conversation. While driving her back to her car,
in my drunken stupor, I drove through a stop
sign colliding with another car.

Things went from bad to worse as I was taken
to jail and booked, while my companion was
taken to a local hospital with minor injuries.
After sobering up at the police station, I called

my wife, asking her to come and bail me out. While she was at the police station, she had the opportunity to read the booking report, including details of the other passenger in my car.

The hardest thing I ever had to do was confess my indiscretions to my wife. A year prior, I'm sure it would have resulted in divorce. However, her newfound faith prompted her to forgive me, but with conditions. She insisted that I join a church group called celebrate recovery. It's very similar to AA but based entirely on biblical principles. I enjoyed the meetings and the camaraderie with the other men in the group. It appeared that my life was coming back together.

Then everything changed. I arrived home from my meeting and found my wife was attending a Bible study that evening, leaving my 12-year-old daughter Carrie to babysit her younger brother. I settled in to watch the ballgame while drinking a glass of orange juice. At that point Satan spoke into my ear. There's beer in the refrigerator in the garage. One won't hurt you. I took the bait and called to my daughter, "Carrie, bring daddy a beer from the garage."

A few minutes later she handed me a Budweiser and said, "daddy, are you sure you should be drinking this?"

"No problem honey, daddy's just gonna have one. With that she walked away with a sad look on her face that I will never forget. I barely swallowed my first mouthful of beer when the taste hit me. It was disgusting. I barely made it to the sink before throwing up. At that point I called my daughter and scolded her severely for putting something in my beer. She denied ever putting anything in the beer, but I did not believe her and told her to go to her room immediately. At this point, I went into my garage, looked in the refrigerator and this time picked up a different brand, a Miller light. I twisted off the cap and took a long swallow, and immediately threw up all over my garage floor.

I never believed much in miracles, but what else could it have been? Why would the taste of the beer be so abhorrent to me? I loved the taste of beer in the past. Then I remembered my friend Bill at celebrate recovery saying to me that God works in mysterious ways. I thought about that the rest of the evening and apologized to my daughter for not believing her.

Fast-forward five years. After that day, I have never even thought of having an alcoholic beverage. A couple of weeks after the incident, I went forward in church and surrendered my life to Christ. Since then, I attended a local Bible college and became an ordained minister. My wife and I became very active in the church, and we have never been happier.

I will finish with this line. Nobody will ever convince me that God did not step in that day and miraculously saved my marriage, if not my life.

May God bless all who read my story.

Ryan M

My earliest recollection at the age of four is playing baseball. I lived in Indiana with my mom, dad and sister who was two years older than me. We were Christians with a basic belief in God but we never attended church regularly. I remember having a very happy childhood with my life centered around playing baseball. My dad was my baseball coach and we played and practiced every day. I began playing on multiple teams and as my game improved, I played on various travel teams wherever possible. By the time I was in middle school I was very, very good. In high school my baseball skills were praised everywhere and articles appeared in the sports section of local newspapers touting the opportunities I would have in college and beyond because I was really that good.

My parents had marital problems and as a result they divorced while I was in high school. I chose to live with my dad because of a tight connection with him being my baseball coach. My days were no longer carefree. The divorce affected me. I was angry and confused. I wasn't close to my mom but felt guilty and it caused me to question my identity. I was a popular kid in a small catholic high school and lived to get the praise of the community. Convinced that baseball was my ticket to success, it was all I identified with.

In my senior year I got caught at a party where there was alcohol and drugs. It should not have affected my position on my team, but it did. The school had a zero-tolerance policy which prevented me from participating. The relationship with my dad was negatively affected by my failure. He was angry and disappointed. I know my dad loved me, but didn't know how to deal with the situation. Without baseball I was totally lost. After finishing high school and one year or so of college my time was spent having fun drinking and experimenting with drugs and before I knew it, it wasn't only just fun, I needed the drugs and alcohol in order to exist.

I moved back in with my dad, joined the plumber's union and worked with him. A dental issue required a procedure and a prescription for pain pills. The pain pills added to my addiction. It was a rough stretch of time. At one point, I must have overdosed because I woke up with my girlfriend and family staring down at me.

This incident led to my first detox facility. It was apparent to me that I was now psychologically and physically dependent on a multitude of substances and my life was spiraling out of control.

One day, a friend in the plumbers' union invited me to his church. I went with him and was surprised to see my mom there. It was a Pentecostal church. The pastor seemed to be looking directly at me and listening to him I found myself weeping uncontrollably the whole time. It occurred to me that God was present as the pastor prayed for me. I was trembling heavily and could barely stand up. It felt that God had saved me, but nothing changed.

At the age of twenty-three I could see no light at the end of the tunnel. Against my dad's advice, I quit the Union, moved to Florida, and soon got involved with "pill mills" and visited every doctor possible to get pain pills. I was dope sick when I tried my first crack cocaine and ended up committing six felonies in order to get the money for more drugs.

I got caught, was sent to jail and prison, receiving a split sentence. After six months they released me on probation for the remainder of my five-year sentence. I entered a Christian rehab facility; but one day walked out along with some girl and ended up injecting crack for the first time. This violated my probation, so I was sent back to prison to finish my sentence.

While in prison my sister sent me my first bible. Prison life allowed me nothing but time to read the bible every day, seeking the Lord, trying to find the reasons behind my addiction. When I was eighteen, I had met Jen, who was a family friend. From the beginning our connection was very special, at least to me. Sitting in prison, she kept appearing into my thoughts and dreams that she would be my wife upon my release. And so it happened, I reconnected with Jen and fell in love. She refused my proposal of marriage, but left the door open in hopes that my addiction was in the past. Her rejection was devastating which led to another relapse.

For the next three years I lived in ten different rehab facilities. Being a driven person, I was impatient and wanted immediate results. It was my opinion that the directors of the facilities did not understand my needs. I knew how to manipulate people to see my way of thinking so I would get released early only to relapse and try a different facility. When the urge to use attacked me, I couldn't trust myself to be alone.

Believing I was improved, I married Jen. She tried to help me and in the first year and a half of our marriage I relapsed seven or eight times. After each failure, I learned something different about myself. Finally, crying out to God, I said, "God why do I keep doing this? I'm a train wreck." I would enter a program, then complete it and relapse again. Later I realized that my lapses always stemmed after a rejection from someone or something because I didn't know where my acceptance came from. I was in bondage to my lack of identity.

Jen had our first child, a son. He was perfection. Yet having everything to live for, I relapsed again. This was the worse time. My six-month old son needed me and I'm a failure. My wife won't speak to me and left me. I've lost my wife and child and all that is left is my wish to end it all. I had serious suicidal thoughts and planned to end my life by jumping from the Florida Sunshine Skyway bridge thus ending this senseless merry-go-round.

Following the recommendation of a friend, I entered a rehab in South Carolina which to me was intolerable. So, I left and went to New Orleans, but they wouldn't take me in due to having left South Carolina. I then sold my car and all my possessions except the clothes on my back and travelling to Indiana to live with my mom. At this point, I truly believed that recovery was impossible. However, my in-laws and my mom never gave up on me. They loved me and tried to help me through all of my messes. So, I found myself yet again going back to the original Christian Recovery Center. This time I entered with a different attitude. I would do everything they wanted me to do, without complaining, without trying to convince them that I knew better, no matter how silly I thought it was. I finally submitted. I had tried everything else without success, so I submitted.

The answer was so simple. After thirty days there, I felt God was radically transforming me. Mom again came to my rescue by sending me money to pay my rent for another thirty days, as I wanted to be assured that I was really changing. I started working two days a week earning money to give to my wife. I was now sixty days sober and on fire for the Lord. One particular day during the sixty days, I was sitting quietly outside holding a mug of black coffee and noticed my reflection in the cup. Staring into the cup, my hands started shaking as it occurred to me what I was looking at. It wasn't seeing a drug addict; it was the image of a transformed child of the living God.

My wife agreed to let me see my son which meant that I would be driving pass the drug house where I used to purchase my drugs. Stopping there never crossed my mind. God had literally and radically transformed my mind. My psychological and physical need to do drugs had been taken away. That was the true miracle. Realizing that my identity is now found in God, I was ready to experience freedom from the bondage of approval and rejection. I no longer needed to seek anyone's acceptance because my acceptance was in God.

I went from being a homeless drug addict to being a happily married man with a resurrected and restored marriage. I am the proud father of an adopted son, a son and an infant daughter. I started my own respectable business from zero dollars to earning $100,000 the first year. The following year my business doubled and this year it has grown again. We purchased our own home. I have been blessed beyond my wildest dreams. My relationship with my dad is restored. He almost gave up on me because he had a dream for my baseball career and when that crashed, he felt he was a failure. He is now 65 years old, living in Indiana, and we share long walks when we get together.

I am still a man driven to succeed. But now, my success is measured in how God is using me now to help others and to be the man, the husband, the dad, and the son I should be in God's plan. I spend time at the rehabilitation center attending the church service and helping the pastor. Recently while reading my bible, my thoughts started wandering until I felt like I was floating and thoughts of what does God want me to do now switched to God asking me, "what do you want to do?" That's silly, I thought, there is no way God is asking me what I want. My purpose; that's what I want. I want to fulfill my purpose which I feel God has called me to. I want to be able to devote more time sharing

God's love and message for a life of freedom to those that suffer in the same way I did. God has revealed to me my true purpose in Christ.

Berk B

1 Peter 5:10 *"And after you have suffered a little while, the God of all
grace, who has called you to his eter-
nal glory in Christ, will himself re-
store, confirm, strengthen and estab-
lish you."*

Acts 2:17: *"And in the last days it
shall be, God declares, that I will
pour out My Spirit upon all flesh; and
your sons and daughters shall prophesy, and your young men shall see visions, and your old men shall dream
dreams."*

Three dreams and one day in 2003

Over the years, I have spent many days study-
ing and sharing the Word of God to as many
people as He put in my path. This included
many trips to Africa delivering Bibles in the native language of the people I am visiting. Also

supporting the Ministers and Pastors in their endeavors to spread the Word of God in their primitive regions. What follows is an account of what happened during my trip to Africa in the year 2003.

Since my age falls between young and old, I feel it reasonable for me to experience varying amounts of Prophesy, Visions and Dreams. In November 2003 I planned another mission trip to Malawi, a country in the eastern part of Central Africa. Prior to my departure I experienced three dreams, which at the time made no sense to me.

In my first dream, I found myself walking down a corridor and was aware of two very large black men dressed in suits following me. I stopped and they continued to walk past me, one on each side. The one on the left turned and faced me, smiling; he bowed one-third at the waist, making constant eye contact with me but saying nothing. At first, I had fear (for their size), then, I felt at peace when he smiled.

In my second dream, I was at an airport looking for my African contact whom I had never met, but had seen a picture. I thought I might have passed him distantly, but continued forward into a denser group of African Nationals, who accosted and heckled me, until a stranger whisked me away to safety, without incident.

In my third dream, I found myself walking in a sparse scrubby bush area approaching an extremely large tree with a rooty base, flaky fibrous bark, similar to a Cypress tree. As I approached, I saw a snake skin before I saw one black snake, about four feet long, and then another. I felt no fear since as a child, I raised snakes. I continued beyond the tree and turned back to see that the tree was filled with four-foot black vipers. One by one the snakes launched at me from the tree and I simply stepped from one side to the other avoiding contact. They died when they hit the ground.

I flew to South Africa proceeding north to Malawi. I successfully met my airport contact, Pastor Stephen Tambuli, a native Malawian with whom I had corresponded. Our missionary group, Joseph's Cupbearers, had provided a truck to Missionary friends of this pastor, which we used for our journey. Pastor Stephen had already procured the requisite insurance, road worthiness certificate, and had his Malawian driver's license. We purchased food and supplies for several days for our stay in the bush country as we planned to minister in different villages. I spent the night in the town of Blantyre, a city founded by the great missionary to Africa, Dr. Livingston.

The next day, one hour after sunrise, we headed southwest for twenty-five miles to a village in Chikwawa to meet with the village leaders. Their small open church was constructed of mud and straw with hard mud benches. It was adorned with bougainvillea blossoms and in its own way was quite beautiful, being the best structure in the village. Many joined us as five men climbed into the back of our truck and four women with two children (a young baby and a suckling pre-toddler) climbed into the back seat of our double cab Toyota 4x4 truck. Most of the men spoke a combination of English and Chechewa, but the women spoke only Chechewa. We continued on, driving several miles, before stopping at a small village to purchase drinks and snacks, as our next church stop would be some ninety or so miles farther south.

After we all settled in, the truck wouldn't start. It appeared that the battery was too weak to start the engine. Push starting it didn't work. Then God answered our prayers. There was a small shop that had a very old, dusty battery charger which worked! Once the battery was charged, we returned our borrowed tools and continued on. These African roads are extremely rough, more like a washboard with ridges and pot holes. However, if you drive a certain speed, the bounce of the tires will dance on top of the ridges and the ride is bearable. The speed to attain this is often between 50 to 65 miles per hour.

We continued driving south another twenty miles, passing an occasional village, when the truck suddenly stopped in the middle of the road. Here we are stranded with 70 more miles to our destination. (Satan never quits) The battery caps were missing and the battery acid had leaked and bounced out on the engine which overheated. We praised God that we were only a little over a mile's walk to a very large village with many stores. We stopped at the police building and were escorted around the village looking for battery acid. Of course, there was no acid. But we walked past a hut and noticed an old battery case. We inquired of its keeper. He had one battery and it looked as though he had personally rebuilt it. We hired two bicycles and the four of us (two villagers on one bike with the battery and I peddling the other with Pastor Tambuli holding on) cycled back to the truck. We removed our damaged battery, replaced it with the "new" battery, (I use that term loosely), turned the key and absolutely nothing happened! We took this battery out, filled the engine radiator and re-installed our old battery. One of the men found a plastic bag by the side of the road, tore it up and shoved it into the open holes in the battery to prevent further acid loss.

I felt the confidence of the LORD and told Stephen to start the truck. He then motioned the men to try pushing again, but I indicated, "no" just turn the key. It started! Praise God! Everyone piled back into and onto the truck and I shouted "Hallelujah!" The fellow native riders laughed and praised God while the women started to sing.

Off we went, three to four hours behind schedule. As we were driving, we passed hundreds of scattered bicyclists, pedestrians and vehicles, and passed within 6-12 inches at speeds that were not exactly slow. At one point we encountered a small child about six years old on a bicycle too large for him, who fell over his bike in the middle of the road. We skidded through the gravel and came to a stop within inches of the bike which was under our left front bumper. A fearful event which, evidently, is not uncommon for the area. The boy was fine and we both continued on our way.

After a time, we left the main road and continued on a trail leading to the village church. We drove as far as we could and then were relegated to walking the rest of the way. Even though we were about four and a half hours late, the people (about 250 in number) cheered as we neared the church. What a blessing! Their commitment, their joyful commitment, was astonishing to me. The people had gathered there with about 15 Pastors from various villages, as far away as the neighboring country of Mozambique. I greeted the Brethren, praised them for their faithfulness as we sang and sort of danced in place praising God. Pastor Stephen spoke on holiness; putting away the fetishes and the mixing of tribal superstitions and relying on the power of God, his Son Jesus (Yesu Christo) and the Written Word of God. I then dedicated and presented brand new KJV Bibles in the Chechewan tongue to each individual Pastor. We prayed for three who came forward. As we walked from the church, the people followed singing praises to God until we reached our truck, which, by the way, fired up without a problem as we started our return trip.

A few miles down the road, the left rear truck tire went flat. Thankfully, we had a lug wrench, the spare was good, and after refashioning a tool, using mosquito spray as a lubricant, we were able to remove the lug nuts. But we had no jack! As I was under the truck, my new friends found three flat rocks to position beneath the axle. They lifted the side of the 4x4, we changed the tire, and were ready to resume our journey. Once again, I shouted, "Hallelujah" and they responded "Hallelujah!"

The country is severely barren due to the cutting of trees by needy people for fuel. As we were driving, I noticed an area with tall trees and bush beside the Shire river, which we had paralleled as we drove many miles. I inquired and was told that evil spirits inhabit that area and blood sacrifices are offered; something also about a snake and a woman. The trees were tall and thick since the people only approach so far in their quest for firewood. . . sort of a line of demarcation between fear and need.

In my heart, I wanted to go there and allow the Holy Spirit to overcome that wicked place.

Malawi is filled with demons and witch doctors, and fear of principalities of darkness, curses, blood sacrifices and witchcraft. A place really in need of the truth and power of God. We didn't stop, but continued on, all fourteen of us as we had one additional rider from the Nsanje village. We passed Bangula, a large village with a grass air strip and permanent buildings. This was mid-way between Bangula and our destination of Chikwawa (about twenty miles), close to a village near the township of Ngabu.

Previously, throughout the day, we had requested for Pastor Stephen to slow down as the men in the back precariously fought being bounced off the truck. Also, I mentioned to him that we should take it easy as we had no spare, had overheated once already, and our battery was energized simply by the grace of God. That's when it happened, our biggest challenge of the day.

We had been following another 4 x 4 truck when it slowed, giving us the opportunity to pass. With the customary horn blow (at 50 mph) we started to pass but two cyclists didn't get over enough causing Stephen to veer slightly, then veer in the opposite direction to avoid hitting the truck we were passing. I calmly asked Stephen to slow down but it was too late. This side-to-side motion culminated in our vigorously rolling the vehicle five or six times. I knew it was coming and the roll started on my open window side. Glass breaking, metal crunching, bodies tumbling inside and outside the truck. On the third roll I realized I was not in any pain and with my eyes open my backpack hit me in the face before it disappeared outside the truck. I closed my eyes between the 4th and 5th roll and hope sparked within my heart, still no pain, and one plea to God, "OK, LORD, you can stop this now;" but no, one more roll. The truck was listing on its side. I unbuckled, crawled out my window and then saw my backpack and picked it up as I approached the side of the road. My first instinct was to get away from the truck and off the road. I turned around only to see a destroyed truck and bodies all over the place; a few barely moving, others still and quiet, and some remaining in the overturned truck.

The driver of the truck we had passed, a Philippine looking man, and his friend ordered me to get in the back of their truck. I was reluctant and refused because the other people needed help. With no other option, I then complied and was able to help the villagers put six other people in the back beside me. One was obviously dead. I prayed for her entrance into heaven, as I comforted another woman who leaned against me for support. As we started to drive away, two or three of the villagers started to accuse me while waving their hands in my face. I was the only white guy; the only one to walk away unharmed. I believe they must have assumed I was the driver. I was driven away safely to a nearby clinic by someone I didn't know, where I helped the wounded into the clinic.

After washing up outside I went to the office of the Ngabu police. It would be a very long night. I walked back to the clinic with the district traffic sergeant where I learned five souls lost their lives that day in the service of the LORD. Pastor Stephen had a broken neck and remained in the clinic for some time. One pastor and his wife had died, along with one of the children. Those that survived, were all physically wounded, except for me. You see, as the vehicle was being twisted by the force of the rolling, a dome in the roof above me was being formed—miraculously so! Other than a minor abrasion on my left elbow, caused by the contact of the road passing by my window during the first roll, I had sustained no injuries. Realizing what I saw, the extent of the damage, injuries and deaths, undoubtedly confirmed that The Grace of God was with me. It humbled me. News spread quickly through the villages as well as the Christians in the City which allowed me to be a living witness and testimony to the goodness of God.

Interpretations to the Three Dreams: The last is first and the first is last.

The snakes launching themselves at me were the principality demons which are great in number in Malawi, because of the worship of dead family members, witch doctors, witchcraft, fetishes and a general sense of superstition and fear. The LORD protected me as I was able to sidestep them by my faith in the power of Christ and the Word of the Almighty God!

The dream concerning Malawians accosting me was fulfilled when the villagers at the accident scene came at me with words shaking fists in my face. I was whisked away in the back of a truck to safety, by someone I didn't know.

The first dream (of the two ten-foot black men in suits) were the angels of God, provided to me to protect me from harm. As the vehicle I was in tumbled, a dome in the roof of the truck above my head was formed to protect me by the Heavenly host. Only I escaped without injury, as five Christian Brethren stepped into Glory and others still suffer severely and suffer to this day.

May this be a memorial to all of those who have given their lives, both in the distant past as well as the recent, for the cause of Christ and for the edification of the saints. May we be inspired by their commitment to seek the LORD more diligently.

Now, may we work for the King, while we still have breath loaned to us by His Grace, unto His Glory, through Christ Jesus His Son. Amen.

Linda M

> Mark 16:15 *"And He said to them, "go into all the world and proclaim the Gospel to the whole creation."*
>
> Matthew 7:13-14 *"Enter by the narrow gate. For the gate is wide and the way is easy that leads to destruction, and those who enter by it are many. For the gate is narrow and the way is hard that leads to life, and those who find it are few."*

I was born with one blind eye and as a two-year-old, almost died in the hospital undergoing a simple tonsillectomy. At the time the doctor predicted I would probably be totally blind before reaching 30 years of age.

My family rarely went to church and my parents then divorced when I was 10. Having no clear direction, I married at a very young age.

In 1965 my husband, Mac, became very ill with chronic obstructive pulmonary disease

(COPD), as well as emphysema. The doctors indicated this would greatly shorten his life and he was expected to only live about a year. That's when I began to contemplate, what happens when a person dies? I had heard there was a place called heaven, and a place called hell, but knew very little about the subject. We all know, however, that death comes sooner or later. My future did not seem to offer much at that time. Being an only child and losing both my parents was devastating. Now I had to face losing my husband. My children Marilyn and Patrick were growing up rapidly and would soon be getting married leaving me alone to face an empty life.

In the summer of 1975, I was desperately searching for a purpose in my life. Having been a professional musician for many years and well respected by my peers in the profession, I was now coasting through life, working only twenty-four hours a week successfully. Someone once said, "Find what you love and you will never work a day in your life." Playing music was my passion, but in spite of all this, there was still an empty void in my life that nothing seemed to fill. Fortunately, unbeknownst to me at that time, the Lord had his hand in my life. Even though my evening hours were spent in pubs, restaurants and nightclubs, I never smoked nor drank alcohol. Seeing myself as a good person, I learned later that Satan is always seeking to kill, steal or destroy.

A popular opinion in the secular world is that Religion may not do a lot of good, but it certainly won't do any harm. Based on that philosophy, I took my two children to a local church and Sunday school. Being exhausted from playing music on Saturday nights and not getting home until 1:00 or 2:00 a.m., I would sleep in my car until the service was over.

One morning, my children told me that the church was offering a class on death and dying. This caught my attention and I decided to sign up for the classes. It was exactly what I needed at the time, not realizing how lost I was. Although I considered myself a good person, I was still a sinner separated from God. I finally learned how much Jesus Christ loves each and every one of us. He came to earth to pay the ransom, bore punishment for our sins to make us right with God.

On August 15, 1975, I confessed to being a sinner and turned my life over to God. I invited Jesus Christ to come into my heart, to be my

Lord and Savior, and to cleanse my heart. This was a turning point in my life. It was the most wonderful experience. Then on March 27, 1976, I was baptized. From that point on, I developed an insatiable desire to learn more about God and to read his word. I was fully committed and enrolled in Bible college for five years for which, God provided the resources that were needed.

Three times in my life, I heard the audible voice of God call my name in the middle of the night while I was asleep. He would call Linda, Linda in the most loving, gentle, deep and peaceful voice. It caused me to sit straight up in my bed to see who was calling me. His voice was that of no other person I'd ever heard. I actually would get up and look around the house and even went outside to see if maybe somebody was out there calling me but there was no one. My family was sound asleep, and I was alone listening to the voice of God calling my name.

A couple years later, while attending Bible school with some lady friends of mine, we went to a healing service in Lakeland, Florida. I told them I wasn't feeling well, and had a very bad sore throat, but these girls insisted that I go with them. As soon as I got in their car, they laid hands on me and prayed for healing of my sore throat. In less than five minutes my throat was totally healed and never did come back. However, my right eye began tearing for no reason at all. I was looking around the crowd of people trying to find some other folks that I may know from church who might be there. But only being able to see a few rows away, everything beyond that was blurry. This caused me a great deal of concern, because it was important for me to be able to drive a car.

As the pastor was teaching, I was taken back by what he said. "Someone here tonight has a serious problem with their right eye and it is watering for no apparent reason, and if that person would stand up, they will be healed." Well, I didn't know if that was me or not, but I wanted to be healed, so I stood up. The pastor, along with others in the room began to pray for me. Several minutes later, while looking around the auditorium, I was amazed that the numbers on a gentleman's jersey way up in front of the church was perfectly visible. I even saw a silver Italian horn necklace on a lady who was sitting on the opposite side of the sanctuary! Well, that was the most exciting time of my life! What a true miracle! After more than fifty years, my eyesight is still fine. In fact, it seems to have even improved.

Over the years, I have experienced many things that most people wouldn't believe. I struggle to believe it myself sometimes, but I have heard the audible voice of Jesus, and have seen a vision of him smiling at me. I could go on and on sharing miracles, but this will suffice for now. May God bless all who have read my story.

John W

Psalm 147:3 *"He heals the broken-hearted and binds up their wounds."*

Hebrews 13:5 *"I will never leave you; nor forsake you."*

I was born in 1946, raised in Northeastern Ohio and attended a private Christian school from first grade through high school. Throughout my life, I've been a faith believer but only once have I had an experience that goes well beyond coincidence. Coincidence is not always a coincidence. It could be the physical proof of God moving in our lives.

I was only five years old at the time but that ten-minute trauma has left me unable to purge it from my memory for the past 70 years. Like most little boys, my curiosity had a way of getting me in trouble. I heard my neighbor Mrs. B's rabbit had babies and I wanted to see them. Without asking my mom's permission, I took it upon myself to go across the road to see the bunnies. Mrs. B had a rabbit hutch next to a shed where she kept chickens. I walked up to the hutch and watched the bunnies nursing for a while. My interest satisfied, I turned to leave when I saw a large hole in the ground full of water. My first thought was maybe it had fish, frogs or tad poles swimming there; something every five-year-old gets excited about.

Back in those days, indoor plumbing was rare out in the country. That hole was in fact a pit intended for a new "outhouse" location. There had been a lot of rain and the pit was nearly full of water. It was my lucky day, I thought, as I spied on the ground an empty soup can which would come in handy to scoop out whatever I was fortunate enough to find in the water. As I stood looking into the pit, I heard a commotion behind me coming from the chicken coop. As I turned to investigate, the wet grass under my foot gave way and I fell into the water-filled pit.

To this day, I can see the wet grass and mud oozing between my fingers, as I clung on for my life. The pit, I learned later, was five feet deep with me being barely three feet tall. The situation was looking extremely bleak. All the screaming didn't help as Mrs. B was very hearing impaired and she was in her house. Her eyesight wasn't much better either. Mrs. B explained to my mother that she went to the kitchen sink and casually glanced out the window. From approximately thirty yards away, she saw my two tiny fists clutching the grass. She hobbled out just in time to pull me out. I can visualize her face and feel her feeble hands on my wrists. I can also very well remember the spanking she gave me before walking me home.

Looking back, it was the most wonderful spanking of my life! It felt good to be held and be alive on dry ground. What possessed her to go to the sink and look out the window? With everything there was to see, what drew her eyes to two tiny fists desperately clutching to life?

The answer is simple, God saw my distress and he compassionately stepped in.

Warren A

1 Kings 19:12 "And after the earth-quake a fire, but the Lord was not in the fire; and after the fire the sound of a low whisper."

In the early 60s I was like every other young man my age. I had always been kinda, sorta religious... Went to church, read an occasional Bible verse, and even put a few bucks in the offering plate. In those days I would be described as brash, a bit self-centered with the smidgen of arrogance. The Marine Corps cured that my first week at Parris Island. With my attitude adjustment complete, I moved on.

I flew F8 fighters off aircraft carriers in the 1960s. One night returning from a mission I had zero visibility. No problem for a hot rock fighter jock like me, Except for one problem, my altimeter malfunctioned. Outside the cockpit in total blackness, I strained to pick up the carriers landing lights. It was then, I heard

that still small voice; "wings level, full power".
In layman's terms, that meant pull up, now.
Instinctively I obeyed, as taught from the first
day at boot camp; instant obedience. Wings
level full power, done.

When I looked back into the cockpit the altimeter showed 60 feet not 600 feet which was
the proper altitude. My instruments showed
descending, not flying level. When I simultaneously leveled the wings and jammed full power,
the fighter jumped. Was I scared? Petrified. No
more hot rock fighter jock. I climbed to 40,000
feet pulled the power to idle, and coasted for
the distant shore, to save precious fuel. By vi-
sual search I found a military airbase, followed
no radio procedures and landed safely.

The landing signal officers aboard the carrier
related to me what they saw of my flight. 'As
your fighter turned toward the ship it began to
descend. The carrier deck is 62 feet above sea
level, but I was flying at 60 feet. The landing
signal officers realized I was going to crash into
the stern of the carrier so they both jumped
off the stern of the carrier into the safety nets
below the deck on Portside. Other fighters in
the past have indeed plowed into the sterns
of carriers and safety nets were placed on all

carriers for the L.S.O's safety. "As we watched for your certain crash, we saw the impossible. It looked like a giant hand pushed your fighter straight up". Not only did I scarcely miss the stern of the carrier but also popped over the 100-foot towering superstructure and upper decks above the landing area on the starboard side of the ship.

That was almost 60 years ago, but I remember it like it was yesterday. After that night, I thanked God every day for showing up when he did. Vietnam was a scary place. I actually wrote a two-word prayer which I repeated almost daily, Yahweh HELP!

Aaron R

1 Corinthians 2:5 "So *that your faith might not rest in the wisdom of men but in the power of God.*"

I am a Christian; born into a Christian Family, one of five siblings. The Bible and our relationship with God have always been the vital core of our lives. When I was ten, my dad held a part-time regional position with the organization, FCA (Fellowship of Christian Athletes). FCA Hockey was re-organizing and my dad felt he could contribute more to advance the message of the organization and interviewed for the open position of Vice President of FCA. Much to our family's shock, my dad was not chosen and we were stunned.

In December 2009 as my dad and mom were praying looking for God's guidance, the verse in Isaiah 6 verse 8 came to light within them, Isaiah's Commission from the Lord: "And I heard the voice of the Lord saying, "Whom shall I send, and who will go for "us?" Then I said, "Here I am! Send me."

My family felt the Lord was leading us into full time ministry; representing FCA while winning souls for Christ. The picture wasn't clear how we were going to accomplish this; a fifty-state tour in the United States, roughly staying and working one month in each state with my parents' home schooling us. August 2011 my parents sold our home, our cars, and most of our possessions. We purchased a 14-foot trailer and a van and started our journey in Maine. My youngest brother was only two months old at that time and as families volunteered to host my family of seven; we travelled across the United States, sometimes staying in the host family's basements, second homes, or as a last resort, renting space. Our tour ended in December 2015 and we returned to Eden, Utah. During those five years, I had missed playing hockey on a competitive level.

In Utah, I was involved in the civil air patrol while chasing my dream of playing competitive Hockey. When I was 16, I was playing Dodge Ball and experienced a shoulder tear; the pain was excruciating, unlike anything I had ever experienced. I stopped playing, waiting two weeks, but it was not improving. I was in a state of anguish, as I had missed five years of hockey and might now miss another hockey season. I tried to play through the pain but it never improved.

The doctor sent me for X-rays and then an MRI which showed that I had a severe tear to the Labrum in my shoulder as well as a large cyst growing there which required surgery and a six-month rehabilitation period after surgery. To multiply our concerns, we were in the process of moving from Utah to Minnesota and we were undecided where to have the surgery performed. My family and I prayed consistently for direction on where, when and who should do the surgery which could affect and possibly determine my hockey performance. We decided I should have the surgery done in Minnesota at the end of summer. Throughout the summer God kept bringing up to me the scripture from Daniel 3: 16-18, wherein the Jews, Shadrach, Meshach, and Abednego were in the fiery furnace but had no fear as they believed God would deliver them out of the situation. In the same manner, I prayed, "God, I believe you can heal me, even if the doctors say it is impossible. I believe you will heal me.

"And if you don't, I believe in you."

The week before surgery, there was a hockey super tournament in Minnesota which I intended to play. As I packed my goalie equipment, I realized I felt great. I felt free from pain and actually won the MVP of the tournament. I told my dad, "Why do I have to have this surgery?" "God has healed me."

My parents were not convinced that I was healed, as the doctors had told them that it was impossible for the labrum tear to heal itself and that the cyst needed to be removed. Our doctor is also a Christian and a personal friend of our family, but he emphatically told me, "Aaron, this can't heal itself, you have to get surgery."

On the way to the hospital, I told my mom, "Mom, promise me that if the doctor goes in there and I am healed, that he won't do anything." My mom agreed to inform the doctor. The surgery was scheduled for one hour and thirty minutes. They gave me anesthesia and prepared to start the procedure.

The doctor approached my mom in the waiting room after a short thirty minutes and my mom panicked thinking, "what's wrong?" The doctor faced my mom and informed her that there was nothing for them to do. The doctor explained that the large tear was completely healed back together in a way that was better than what they would have been able to accomplish with surgery. The cyst was also completely gone with only a minimum trace of tissue. He told my mom that I had been miraculously healed and that he had no scientific explanation to what he saw in my shoulder.

When I woke up, my parents and I and the doctor compared the pictures of the before and after. The doctor told me, "Aaron, you were correct, God healed you. I have no other explanation."

I am now twenty years old; I am still pain free and have full range of motion in my shoulder. I'm a hockey goalie playing in the top junior league in the United States, while faithfully committed to play for the Air Force Academy in the next year.

My prayer for you is that if you are facing a challenging situation, medical or not, that you will faithfully and continuously pray for God's guidance and healing. Because we know this to be true, as in **Matthew 19:26** , *"With man this is impossible, but with God, all things are possible."*

Shawn P

My mom was a heroin addict and not much was known about my dad. I was told by my mom while she was high on heroin that he had been shot in the head and died before I was one year old. My start in life was rocky in New Jersey, just across the river from New York. My mom used narcotics for the entire time of her pregnancy and I was born addicted and in critical condition. My heart had stopped several times while being incubated. Upon release from the hospital my grandparents were given custody by Court Order.

I was born Catholic. My grandmother was of German descent and a tough disciplinarian in a devout catholic family. She had a difficult time coping with my mom moving in and out of the picture and her constant drug use. My grandfather was also an alcoholic and an abuser of everyone in the home.

My earliest recollection that our home situation was far from normal was during my early childhood years. I realized that the sexual and physical abuse at the hands of my grandfather was far from normal. During this time, I attended a Catholic School and Church as well as serving as an altar boy. I was already becoming rebellious being filled with anger and hurt inside from all the abuse. Even though my grandmother was tough, she couldn't handle me. I would come and go from the house at will and had already started drinking alcohol and smoking pot by the age of eleven.

At fourteen, I moved in with my mother and half-brother who became my responsibility. He was ten years younger than me and I would often cut school in order to take care of him since my mom had not overcome her serious addiction to narcotics. At fifteen, my mom died of an overdose in my arms. She had been trying to cook a Thanksgiving Dinner and we had a vicious argument about how unfit a mother she was to my brother and me. I carried guilt and regret over her death feeling that my words had contributed to her overdose.

Again, the court stepped in. My brother went to live with his father and I was returned to the home of my grandmother. I can only remember being filled with uncontrollable anger, guilt, and grief at the loss of my brother and mother. My grandmother and I had a lot of conflict. One time in an uncontrollable rage, I hurled the TV through the window which resulted with her calling the police. I was placed in a detention center for two weeks and then transferred to a permanent shelter. After six months and many escapes, at fifteen years and six months I felt that I didn't need anybody. I was a rebellious, angry person. I always believed in God but church had no effect on my life at that time. I had become head strong and street-wise and was removed from the shelter. Being brought before the Judge, I expressed to him I did not want to live in the shelter and could take care of myself. So, the Judge relented and allowed me to live on my own even though I was not quite sixteen. I stayed at the homes of friends or anywhere I could place my head.

Many nights my friends and I would drive over to New York to pick up drugs. This particular night the majority of the guys didn't go. This one guy kept pushing me to join him. He had made some enemies by not paying for some of his drugs. I most always went along with him but this time something told me, don't go. I learned the next day that he was shot in the face and arms by automatic weapons that had also riddled the car seat where I would have been sitting. I know today that God had not given up on me and was protecting me from myself.

I had a high school sweetheart and her family took me in until I was seventeen at which time I moved in with my step-father. He was a kind, caring and all-around good guy even though he was a functioning alcoholic and used drugs. Around that period of time, God had another message planned for me. One evening while leaving a Newark, New Jersey club and standing on the side walk surrounded by several friends, a drive-by shooting occurred. I was standing in the middle, when all the friends around me were shot and wounded but by a miracle, I escaped unharmed. The distinctive sound of bullets whizzing past my head haunted me for a long time.

Two months prior to high school graduation, I was expelled due to fighting and gambling and the next year my step-father, after 35thirty-five years of using drugs, decided to get clean and do it cold-turkey. He spent three days in a detox center, then moved into a half-way house in Florida.

I stayed living in his rental house in New Jersey working various jobs to survive. At the age of twenty-one I left New Jersey, moved to Florida, reunited with my step-dad, and studied and received my GED. However, I was still drinking and gradually moved from smoking pot to prescription drugs.

At twenty-four I met a girl, got serious and was married for seven years. We had no children and both of us were addicted to pain meds. This life style eventually took its toll on us; she cheated on me, got pregnant by her boyfriend, and in a whirlwind of anger, anxiety, abandonment issues, I left her, moved out and started selling pills to survive.

The following year I landed a great job and kept it for seven years. I travelled renovating and remodeling hotels across the country. I was single, my rooms were paid for, my food was provided and I was free to party every night. My alcohol of choice was scotch and I began drinking it like water. I also overdosed five times and five times I was miraculously brought back. God had a hold on me and despite my reckless life style, he was not abandoning me.

January 18, 2016 while remodeling a hotel, I was so high and drunk that my boss finally had had enough and fired me. He had reached the point because I was steadily sinking lower and lower. So, after 38 years of living, I had no money, was homeless, and three quarters of my family were dead. I wanted my life to end. I felt I had already lived my life and seen everything possible. I seriously wanted to commit suicide and began praying to God. "God, take my life. I'm done. God take this pain away. Make this pain stop. If you are who you say you are, help me."

I was crazy drunk and high and was picked up by the Jacksonville Police Department who tased me and took me to a Psycho Ward. After three or four days, homeless and sober, I was still resisting and didn't want the hospital to release me. They were forced to call security due to my yelling and combative behavior. At the same time the police were bringing in another patient who began yelling back at me, "Go to Set Free Ministry," and kept repeating it.

Again, I felt God was answering my plea for help. I called Set Free Ministry and begged to be allowed to stay there but was told there was no room. I became persistent and kept calling until they finally let me come and sleep on the floor. I had $126 to my name for the cab ride. I had come to a time of decision. One hundred twenty-six dollars would buy plenty of liquor and my dope dealer was only around the corner. I chose the cab ride.

Six hours a day, six days a week, spending time in the Bible during this six-month program gave me my life back. I became convinced that God had a purpose for my life and that I had value. That day, January 18, 2016, I was a broken man when I prayed for God to take my pain away, and he gave me my miracle, a home at Set Free Ministry and a pastor to teach me about God's love. I was trusted to participate in work details and my three-month program turned into three years of overseeing the recovery program and teaching classes. I finally had a family of seventy-five people who cared for me. God also softened my heart and I was no longer filled with anger. God had saved me to live a safe life, making money and helping other people. I had totally surrendered my life to Christ and my rewards were boundless. Alcohol and drugs were a thing of the past. I was able to find a temporary place in St. Petersburg, Florida at a Christian transformation enter working and volunteering. My prayers were answered beyond anything I could have expected or imagined. After a time, I moved into my own apartment, continued to volunteer while I'm enjoying my family, church and working as a full-time plumber.

My step-dad, now 64 years old and living in St. Petersburg with my step-mom was fighting liver cancer. God also had a miracle for him; he was accepted and received a liver transplant and is now one hundred percent healed as well as twenty-seven years clean and sober. Our relationship is totally restored.

Artus

Job 12:10 *"In his hand is the life of every living thing and the breath of all mankind."*

Proverbs 19:21: *"Many are the plans in the mind of a man, but it is the purpose of the Lord that will stand."*

In the year 1961, I was a 22-year-old college graduate with aspirations and dreams of moving upward and onward. I met a man who impressed me like no one I had met before. He was four years older than me and seemed so much more mature and sophisticated unlike the boys I had dated in the past. I found his eccentricities charming, reading Winston Churchill's life story, going to foreign movies, listening to radio Moscow on a short-wave radio. His favorite evening pastime was sipping on a Cuba Libra in a German rathskeller, while listening to the Latin band that played there. From time to time, he joined them playing the maracas. Once married, I began to notice things that went beyond the normal idiosyncrasies. He would do a "white glove" inspection of our apartment routinely to make sure there was no dust, or heaven forbid, spots in the kitchen sink. Every, and I mean every, night before retiring he would brush each suit and sport coat hanging in the closet with a whisk broom and shine each pair of expensive dress shoes. He owned no sneakers or casual shoes. His shirts were all laundered with extra heavy starch and returned hanging on hangers.

Without elaborating any further, I will simply say that there were other things that gave me cause for concern. One day he simply informed me that he would never have children. One Friday after eleven months of marriage, I returned home from work to find that his reading chair and lamp, books, short-wave radio, and all of his clothes and personal effects were gone. Suffice it to say, that from that point on, I was living in a kind of fog. Shortly after his departure, the phone calls began, at work, and at home in the middle of the night. The purpose of his calls was never clear; but I was becoming seriously frightened by them. One night there was a knock on the door and as I opened it a crack to see who it was, he shoved against the door trying to push his way in. Unknown to him, I had installed a heavy safety chain after he moved out and it held, although it damaged the wood frame. As he stepped back in surprise, I slammed the door shut.

I didn't wait any longer but immediately found a lawyer and filed for divorce. I was now ready to start living a normal life again. There was a young man, my age, at the company where I worked and like me, he was married but was separated and had a two-year old daughter. He was staying with another single man who had a lady friend and the four of us started going out together. It was a confusing time for both of us and although we really liked each other, neither of us had any serious intentions. Although our relationship gradually became intimate, we realized that we weren't in love with each other.

It was during this time that my former boss was setting up a business out of town and offered me a better job at a higher salary. Even though it meant a 35 mile drive each way, I accepted the position. In the back of my mind, I ignored the signs that I may be pregnant and never saw a doctor. Three months into my new job on a Friday afternoon, I was alone at work. My boss had left the office in the company of the other two men from our office for an afternoon of golf. It was then that I began bleeding, quite heavily, and it didn't stop. I couldn't leave, I had no keys to lock up the office. Frightened, I called my girlfriend. As she was trying to find a way to get me help, my boss, for some reason, came back to the office early. When I told him I thought I was having a miscarriage, he didn't hesitate to help me in his car and rushed me to the hospital. As it turned out, I didn't miscarry, but was in for a very difficult pregnancy. Against the doctor's orders, I continued to work as I had no other option.

I dreaded having to tell my parents about my pregnancy; however, they never wavered in their support. They came up with a plan for me to live in a home for unwed mothers under my maiden name in a city where my dad would be working on assignment toward the end of my pregnancy. The cost of this would be borne by me alone. I had to sell my car, my furniture and most everything and the baby would be placed for adoption. Only my two closest friends, my sister and my parents knew of my pregnancy.

I never told the child's father. The reason was I lived in dreaded fear that this news would find its way back to the man I was still legally married as the divorce was not yet final and the consequences were unthinkable.

I gave birth to a son and as my life turned out, this was the only child I would ever have. I was born a Catholic and had stipulated that I wanted him to be raised by a Catholic family. Throughout the years, I thought of him often and prayed that he was having a good life. Yes, there were many times when I thought of trying to find him, but never did so. I knew the adoption records were sealed, but beyond that, there was no way I would do anything to cause pain to him or his adoptive parents.

In 2005, after retiring from my job, and having a lot of excess time on my hands, I took to exploring the internet and stumbled upon a site for locating lost relatives. On an impulse, I entered the following;

"Son, born November etc. listing the day and year with the name of the hospital and city." Years went by and I completely forgot I had done this.

On January 27, 2015, while checking my emails, I came across an email from a sender

I did not recognize. It was on its way to the trash bin when curiosity got the better of me. I opened it and saw that it was from the site I had registered with ten years before. There was an attachment, which read, "Dear Miss. . . . . , my name is Steve. . . . ., and I think I might be your grandson."

It took me twenty-four hours to digest this; could it be a hoax? I called my sister, the only person living now that knew of my pregnancy and the adoption. She cautioned me not to become too excited, as if I could be anything else!

I answered his email the next day and asked two questions. The first was what was his grandparent's religion? And second, what were their occupations? This was the only information I had been given concerning them. Both answers came back, rapid fire, and they were accurate. I then asked if his father was still living, and my grandson replied in the affirmative. He also told me that I had a total of five grandchildren. He gave me his dad's phone number and I gave him mine; but said I would rather wait until the next day as I needed some time to get my emotions under control. That night, however, when my phone rang at 9:30 p.m., I knew exactly who it would be, and so I spoke with my son for the first time on January 28, 2015. It was unbelievable, well beyond surreal.

I learned that after his adoptive mother passed away in 1996, he tried for years to find me, but was never successful in getting past the iron door. The agency was very steadfast in maintaining privacy for both parties.

Two months later on March 27, my son, Steve, flew to Tampa, and I picked him up at the airport.

Here are some points to ponder:

1. Why did my boss come back early from his golf game when he had never done that before?

2. Why did I not miscarry as the doctor said I could, if not bedridden?

3. When my son was born, I had named him Thomas on his birth certificate.

4. Unknown to me his adoptive father was named Thomas.

5. My son's adoptive father and mother re-named him, Stephen. Spelled Stephen and not the other spelling, Steven.

6. I have one brother, named Stephen. My father's name is Stephen, and so was my grandfather.

7. Why did I find and register on that particular site?

8. What made my grandson take up the search after my son had failed?

9. What made my grandson go to that particular site?

10. Why did I retrieve my grandson's email which I originally intended to trash?

The answer is simple: divine intervention; it had to be. God had a plan for my life far above what I ever thought possible. For many years of my life, I kept drifting away from the Lord, but the Holy Spirit kept drawing me back. Through the years, I had lived with an emptiness in my heart, often dreaming what could have been. By the grace of God, I now have a large family, beyond anything I could have dreamed. My reward was great!

Larry C

Why Friday the thirteenth is one of my favorite days!

Eleven years ago today, I was sitting in the hospital waiting for them to call me back and start prepping me for nine hours of surgery. My friends were sitting with my wife, Cindy, so that when the news came, she would not be alone. Her sister, Sandra, was also there for the inevitable: to comfort Cindy when the bad news came. The statistics told us that I had a fifty-fifty shot at surviving the surgery and a fifty-fifty chance of surviving the two-week hospital stay thereafter. Assuming I survived that, the survival rate was about two to four percent.

When I was called back, there really was no fear or concern: only peace. The staff went about their work and I got hooked up to two IVs (ultimately, I had four, one in each appendage). The surgical suite was extremely cold, and they were playing country music (not my favorite). After commenting about both, they gave me a warm blanket for the cold and told me they could change the music if I wanted, but the surgeon loved this music. I was an instant fan. Next came the epidural and then the all too familiar anesthesiologist explaining what I was about to feel. I frankly don't remember if he asked me to talk or to count backwards, like they often do, but it took about two seconds before the room started spinning on an axis. I was out.

My next memory was waking up to see my wife and Charlie Ray. I have to tell you that I was the most surprised person in the world at that moment, because I wasn't really expecting to survive. I was happy to still be here and for the opportunity I was given at life. I don't remember anything else about that moment, though stories abound about the silly things, though not incriminating, that I said: "There's my brother from another mother" as an example.

The recovery since then has been slow. I have gone from being barely able to walk half a block, to running my first 10K race; from being unable to take the top off of a water bottle by myself, to deadlifting 275 pounds; and many more improvements. Every day is a new adventure and I give thanks to all those who have given me this opportunity. Make no mistake, I am not the person I was at age fifty-four when these cancers hit: and I never will be. I have accepted the fact that I will be anemic, have to sleep on an incline, can't sleep for more than a couple of hours at a time, and the fact that I am in pain all day, every day. But I don't dwell on those things or the fact that I can get violently ill for eating one bite too much. I do dwell on the fact that I again woke up, and rejoice in that. I dwell on being able to do what I can and adapting to the restrictions. I dwell on developing relationships and making new friends, as you can't have too many of those. I dwell on experiencing all that this life has to offer and loving on people, because we are all valuable and worth the investment of time and effort. In short, I rejoice in being alive and I am trying to make the most of it.

Let me go back to those odds that started this story. Some people would dwell on how bad they were and how they were not in my favor. Some people would have given up. Some people would have looked at the survival rate and gone through the treatment not really believing it would work. I admit that when I first got the diagnosis and prognosis, I was devastated. I was at the top of my career, had attained every goal I set for myself and had just regrouped from the devastation of Hurricane Katrine five years earlier.

After wallowing in self-pity for a day and a half, I remembered a promise: my God's promise. At that moment, I admitted I could not handle the truth of my situation and called on my Savior to deal with it for me. I wasn't asking to live, though I wanted to, I was simply turning my problems all over to God because HE promised to deal with them for me. I instantly had peace, and have had that peace ever since. I stopped feeling sorry for myself and stopped dwelling on the negative: I suddenly saw the positives and rejoiced in those as I was still waking up every day and still had an opportunity to impact the lives of others in a positive way. It's all in your perspective and where your faith is.

As this is my eleventh re-birthday, I have a gift for each of you: live, love and laugh. Live life the way it is meant to be lived. Take time to delight in the small things and make yourself a little better each day. Love others, no matter who they are or what they look like or believe: my faith does not give me an option on this point. (Frankly, loving on people is so much easier than hate, which will destroy you from the inside out). Laugh at everything including yourself (which is hard for me sometimes). Get rid of the negatives (including people) and surround yourself with positives, things and people you enjoy and that help you to laugh and enjoy this gift, life, that you have.

Life is fleeting and can be taken from you in an instant. Don't waste it hating, complaining, doing negative things or having negative thoughts. Give thanks, as I do, for your faith, friends and family: they, and you, are worth enjoying and experiencing to the fullest.

I can't express just how happy I am to still be here. I thank God for the opportunity to start over each day. And remember, no matter how bad you think it is, and it may be, there is always hope. As long as you are alive, you have a chance to change things in your life and the lives of others. Don't give up. Get help. Forgive and forget. Rejoice and find your peace. Give of yourself to others and you will be amazed at how good it makes you feel. And last, but certainly not least, LOVE ONE ANOTHER. Just don't give up.   Do random acts of kindness today in celebration of your life and mine.

Thanks for reading.   God bless and have a great rest of your life.   I JUST CAN'T BE-LIEVE IT'S BEEN ELEVEN YEARS, THANK YOU LORD!

Acknowledgments

We would like to thank John Rehg of Soul Attitude Press, for his invaluable assistance in the publishing of this book.

A special thanks to all the many selfless people who took the time to share their life stories and miracles with us.

May you, the reader, also experience the grace and love of our savior, Jesus Christ, as you pray for miracles of healing, forgiveness and peace in your own lives.

About the Authors

Dan's career spanned many years in Sales and Marketing in the Food Service Industry traveling throughout the United States. Dan served as Vice President of Sales and Marketing with several national and international firms. With his wife, Susan, they founded Gulfstream Marketing, a food brokerage company in Florida.

In 1998 at a Billy Graham Crusade in Tampa, Florida, Dan and Susan surrendered their lives to Jesus Christ. After retiring, Dan attended Moody Bible Institute and became an ordained minister serving incarcerated inmates and volunteering at a Homeless Mission.

Dan's love of writing began when he was a young man composing song lyrics and poetry and culminated with the debut and publication of his first thriller novel, "The Cost of Living", in the Spring of 2019. With the success of his first novel behind him, Dan and Susan collaborated on their second novel, "Inherited Destiny," based on a true story.

In this, our third book, we wanted to share with our readers the miraculous life experiences of some ordinary people. "Then God Stepped In" is a compilation of miracles told by the people who experienced them. Our prayer is that all who read this book will be blessed. Visit our website: huntingtonnovels.com

One hundred percent of the sale proceeds of this book will be donated to charity.

www.ingramcontent.com/pod-product-compliance
Lightning Source LLC
Chambersburg PA
CBHW060759050426
42449CB00008B/1454